COLLATERAL *Beauty*

Collateral Beauty
Copyright © 2022 by Rachel Punneo
Edited by Oller Publishing & Co.
Cover and Layout Design by Cheryl Chaney

All rights reserved. No part of this book may be reproduced or transmitted in any form or by any means without written permission from the author.

RACHEL PUNNEO

Prologue:

Welcome to my cancer journey! Spoiler alert: it ends well! The book you're about to read is really my Dear Diary. I've never written anything like this before, but I knew as I was going through this that I didn't want to forget the details of my rollercoaster ride. I didn't want to forget a single act of God's goodness through this process and how He works all things together for the good of those who love him. Romans 8:28. So I started writing things down and it turned into this piece of work right here. I used a popular online photo book making company and had a book that I absolutely treasured. I was happy with that. I even had all those people involved in my journey sign it. The elementary school teacher blood runs deep. I wanted those who had prayed me through this (my doctors, my chemosabes) to be able to put their official stamp on it because they were all very much a part of my healing. I kept it close as my reminder of God's love for me, but had zero plans for it beyond that steadfast reassurance.

Several months later, Carri Oller, a former mom (Her sweet girl is now an eighth grader. I had her in fourth grade.) who recently started her own publishing company asked if I was interested in writing a book about my journey to encourage others and possibly help them on their journey. She pulled the "Pray about it" line. That night I'll be darned if I didn't read Psalm 107:2a. "Let the redeemed of the Lord tell their story." You know I gave God a look on that one. I told Carri I kind of already had written a little something and I would let her read my journal. Once she assessed my writing she could take back any offers guilt free if she wanted. That didn't happen. Instead, we decided to leave it as is (clarifying on relationships here and there and taking out about 200 pictures! I've always said pictures are my love language.) and simply add in some spots for personal reflection. It's a great story, but seeing yourself in it and being able to make your own reflections and pull your own insight from it is what will further your own journey the most. I'm hoping my story can help you. I'm hoping you can catch the joy that comes from a life lived with God as your anchor no matter the circumstances.

I hope my story can shine the light of hope on yours. I hope you can learn to seek out the collateral beauty in poor situations. I believe with the right attitude and relationship with God, you can get through the hardest times in life with grace, love, peace, grit, and moxie. Maybe by seeing someone go through what is your new unknown, you can gain the courage to lean into it, lean on God, and make it through yourself. Maybe even a little better for wear. The statement "I'm better off healed than I ever was unbroken." by Beth Moore is true when you let it be. I hope you enjoy this journey and that the light of the Lord shines through straight to your heart.

Thank you to the many people involved in helping me through the journey and the publishing process!

SEPTEMBER 14

Monday, September 14 with this text is when it all officially began. I started cramping (having another episode) an hour or so before this, but this was the first time I could articulate to Luke, my son, what was happening so he could text for help. My husband, Chris, wasn't answering because he was on a conference call at the time. I got a hold of my doctor first. She said Mercy appointments were over for the day and I needed to go to the ER for any scans I needed. We ended up going to Oklahoma ER and Hospital which I love. They don't charge teachers for services because of their "Heroes" discount, but that was only one of the blessings I experienced that day.

If we back up a bit, this was my 4th episode as I would call them. Each episode brought severe cramping, then 5 days of bed rest while it progressively got better to the point I was completely fine again.

The first came March 23. It was really similar to other digestive episodes I have from time to time, so I thought it was maybe just a longer, more dramatic take on that. May, right before Mother's Day, came another episode that took me out for about 5 days as well. I promised myself then, if this was becoming a thing, I would get myself to the doctor to get this checked out. This sucked. I didn't want to make it a habit. June brought the 3rd episode, and I made an appointment with the doctor. By the time I got in, the pain had subsided some. We took x-rays, bloodwork, and urine samples, but didn't find anything too alarming. Some levels were off, but improved a couple days later. The next step was to do a CT scan. I opted to not do it then because they were crazy expensive, and I was pretty

sure my infection or whatever was gone at that point and probably wouldn't be noticeable. I told her I wanted to be able to get scanned in the thick of it, that she needed to have me signed up for a scan at a moment's notice so we could catch whatever this was at its best.

The Saturday night before this 4th episode we had our annual camping trip to the backyard. Alexis, my daughter, and Apollo and Titan, my grandpuppies, came over to spend the night too. Sunday morning, I woke up to Titan pouncing on the spot that the pain always radiates from, right square on it. I grimaced, but it subsided quickly. The day went on, but I began to tire over the course of shopping for Luke's school clothes. We were heading back to in person school and never got him anything in August.

The next morning, Monday, September 14, I knew I was feeling too exhausted to be normal. With COVID 19 all around, I wanted to be extra cautious so I called in to my principal, Amy, to ask if I could teach from Zoom at home today. She agreed. I barely made it through my zoom classes that day. I turned off my camera at times to lay my head down. I zoomed in a RtI meeting that afternoon after a nap. It wasn't until 4 or so that the debilitating cramps started, and I knew exactly what was wrong with me and it wasn't COVID 19.

As Luke texted the previous text, I was in a bath he had drawn for me because that tended to help in episodes past. One of the first blessings to come of this was that Luke was home doing virtual school and was able to help send the SOS and coordinate all that needed to be. Alexis was my next blessing. She was the first one to reach me. She came in out of breath, so I know she was worried and doing everything she could just to get to me. She gently but firmly helped me out of the bath and into my clothes. I realized then what a blessing it is to have my very own CNA who knows how to move me and dress me in such a professional and loving way. I've truly had the best treatment from the very first second. A minute or two later my mom showed up, the perfect second person. She drove me. I knew if anyone could get me there quickly, it was her. We finally got a hold of Chris. He was able to get to the hospital first, fill out my paperwork, give directions to others, and prepare the way for me. I got in as fast as I did because we weren't able to reach him first to come get me. God's fingerprints are all over this night.

I got to the hospital, saw him, and cried. I hated having to do this, call everybody to arms, and have them worry about me. And I hurt.

Within minutes, I was back in a room, talking to the doctor, giving a urine sample, getting an IV, CT scan, and back in my bed. This hospital really is wonderful. It wasn't long after that, the doctor came in to tell us they saw a mass on my right ovary. They thought it was about 5-6 cm long and he thought it was cancerous. I was so relieved. I know Chris was having the opposite reaction beside me, but I think I even smiled. They found something. I wasn't making it up. There is something to focus on now, something to fix. I asked the doctor again. You found something there?

Again, he said yes. He wanted to transport me by ambulance to OU where they had the best gynecological oncologists around. He was going to set that up, contact my OBGYN, and get back to us. I texted Amy to let her know I wouldn't be in tomorrow. OU ended up being full and was redirecting patients elsewhere that night. I wasn't going there then. He called in an ultrasound tech and that night I had a vaginal and belly ultrasound. The doctor told me to go to my OBGYN the next day and she would refer me to OU. So, we left that night. As we entered the parking lot hours later, everybody was still there. My mom, my in-laws, and the kids were all waiting in the car. COVID procedures wouldn't allow them in the hospital. We headed out in search of food. After pulling into a closed McDonald's on Main St. and Chris backing out of the parking lot because he saw a black cat he refused to cross paths with, we made it home. We hugged each other a little bit tighter, and we went to sleep.

SEPTEMBER 15

My sister, Kortney, called on her way to work and prayed over me. Talk about a sob fest. Chris, her, and I were a mess. There are few prayers I love more than hers. Mom came over so she could take me to my OBGYN whenever I was able to get in. From 7:30am on, I called in every half hour until they let me in. The lady up front was not feeling me with her "I'm sorry, but the doctor's all booked up today."

"Well, call her and get it approved because I'm coming in today. I'll call you back in a half hour to confirm." This was one of the first times of many I proved to be my own best advocate and wouldn't take no for an answer. That was new for me, but a skill I now practice often.

After several calls, the receptionist finally got the doctor's message to get me in today. My appointment was at 12:15 and we had time to rest before leaving. Another blessing in disguise was that Oscar, our dachshund of 18 years, had passed a couple months earlier and Chris and I cleaned the house throughout so that my asthmatic mom could come over and enjoy herself for as long as she wanted. This day was the first in years that she came over, was able to stay for hours, and had no problems.

While there, in her nervousness I'm sure, Mom took the opportunity to clean my fridge and reorganize it to match hers. I may have made an offhand comment days before while standing in front of her fridge, that we needed to have matching fridge organization so that I would know where her things went. Of course, she changed mine when the opportunity presented itself. The funniest thing was that she took all the sauces from fast food places, put like condiments in baggies, found a Tupperware container, and filed them alphabetically in it, Arby's sauce first. I'm the only one I know that has a filing cabinet for their fast-food remnants. She was so into it, I had to tell her we had to go to the appointment. The fridge could wait until later.

Mom couldn't go in with me. Stupid COVID. When I got there the nurse was so nice. She was amazed that my blood pressure and heart rate were so normal. The doctor came in and was very excited for lack of a better word. She said she made me an appointment because they had the best ultrasound lady in the office today and she wanted me seen by her. Another blessing. My doctor was flabbergasted by this. I had just seen her in June right after my last episode. She didn't find anything then. She specifically told me during a very painful physical exam that she would've caught this if it were there in June because it was so large. There was no way she would miss that even if she had no idea it was there.

During my second vaginal ultrasound in 24 hours, this lady really played with this mass, pushing, poking, moving it, etc. The OBGYN and this ultrasound tech were talking back and forth like two excited schoolgirls. I wasn't entirely following everything they were saying. I caught what they wanted me too though. I would most definitely need surgery to take this out. I couldn't do it laparoscopically. There would be a wide incision. I shouldn't return to work due to the fact I could twerk it again causing the pain. She explained it was like a water balloon hanging from a tree. If it got twisted due to moving funny, it would twist, cutting off the blood supply to it. My right ovary thought it was having a "heart attack" and caused pain. I would have to do some more testing, mainly some bloodwork to get my CA125 levels. If it was elevated I would be sent to OU for them to do the surgery. If it wasn't, she would do the surgery. They also said the mass was 10-11 cm, not 5-6.

I had my bloodwork done, but I couldn't help but ask the doctor more and explain that I would feel fine in a few days' time. I was scared that if it disappeared last time in June at my annual appointment just a few days after my last episode, it might not be there in a few days. I wasn't sure if I made that clear, so I stayed and waited to talk to the doctor again. The ultrasound lady came by and asked if I was ok. I told her I had a question for the doctor. I told her this was a crazy question, but is there any way this would go away on its own? She looked at me with such sadness and said "No, this isn't something that will take care of itself." I told her I wasn't worried about fixing it. I was worried it would disappear and we wouldn't be able to remove it. It seems silly she had to explain it wasn't going anywhere, but when she did, it made me feel better and I left hoping it would stick around even though I knew all the pain would soon dissipate. The biggest problem was that the CA125 levels would take several days to get back. She said she would rush the results and call me even if they came in on the weekend. She was a big advocate for me, and I appreciated it. I called Amy to tell her I couldn't go back to school for 6-8 weeks and Chris when I got in the car. I was off to home again waiting for results and the pain to subside. Waiting became the staple of the next several months. Tawnie, my sister-in-law, and I claimed the titles of cyst-ers since she had issues with these as well and laughed about making shirts.

My job also posted today. That was a little hard to look at when I opened my email. There was no doubt who would be perfect but asking Mrs. Valerie to sub for 8 weeks virtually/ maybe in person/who knows in a pandemic where nothing is normal, and everything is hard isn't an easy sale. Amy wanted me to call her. I did. She asked about what I was going through since she worked in gyn onc previously or gynecological oncology. Mrs. Valerie is always a knowledgeable person when you need her in 2020. She was there earlier this year when I broke down at school because of the unexpected loss of Baby Jack, my nephew. She was also a high-risk labor and delivery nurse. When she said she would do it despite previously deciding she wasn't subbing this year, I broke down. I've never cried like that before, but the flood of emotions came, and I couldn't even reiterate to her to think about it overnight. What a gesture. What a sacrifice. I was so moved and humbled, and grateful beyond words.

September 16

While we were praying for quick results, we decided to have our group over for a "sorry to scare you, but thanks for hanging out in the ER parking lot all night" cookout. Chris grilled burgers and dogs. I did nothing. In fact, I had some laminated scales for school I hadn't cut out yet. Everybody decided to cut those out after dinner too. I watched while Alexis gave me a foot rub. The support I've been shown is second to none.

SEPTEMBER 17

My CA125 results came in and they were elevated which meant I had to be referred to OU Gynecological Oncology. She reiterated that this doesn't necessarily mean anything, but she would rather they handle it since they are the experts. My OBGYN had already sent a referral and was telling them to hurry up. I was OK with this. As I was praying over the course of the past few days I realized I wanted to be referred to OU. I was getting the surgery either way. I might as well have the best of the best operating on me. Prayer 1: quick results. Check. I was happy to receive this news and started praying for the exact doctor God needed me to have. If they didn't call me by tomorrow, I needed to call in the morning. I was on it. I contacted a pharmacist friend from OU to see if she knew who the best doctors were in this department. She wasn't sure.

SEPTEMBER 18

A family friend's fiancé was working an angle for us we hadn't even realized at first. She manages one of the cancer departments at OU and was willing to get us in with the best there was. We had been praying for the best doctor to take care of this and this was one obvious way He was delivering on that. I don't think if OU had been accepting patients the night of the ER, I would have ended up in Dr. Jackson's care. I needed to wait on God's timing. He was preparing the way. I called OU's Gynecological Oncology department and got word that while Dr. Jackson wasn't typically taking new patients, she would be my doctor. They told me how amazing she was, and I felt so blessed to have her on my side. Prayer 2: God approved doctor, Check! We were now on to saying big prayers for her, her passion for her patients, ability to problem solve, peacefulness, knowledge, health, happiness, and so much more. I had an appointment for Wednesday and was looking forward to it.

Mom came over and made an amazing charcuterie board because I just wanted to nibble. I have never wanted for anything because of the amazing people around me.

That night Amy sent out communication to my kids and parents which was nice. Mrs. Valerie sent it to me so I could see it. My people are the best at taking care of me!

SEPTEMBER 19

After a whirlwind week, I just wanted to spend some quality time with my 14-year-old, Luke. We sat and watched some shows, tried a new recipe for cinnamon apples (They were amazing!), and just rested in each other's company.

One of my teaching colleagues texted me and gave me some of the most reassuring news ever.
She, for some weird reason, ordered two shirts of our 4th Grade Strong tees a couple weeks prior. I had no idea why. Neither did she though she knowingly did it. In this text, she said it was going to the perfect home, Mrs. Valerie. I couldn't believe it. God knew this was going to happen. God even prepared the way for Valerie to be 100% part of our team. He cares about the details. If He cared enough to take care of this, I knew I had nothing to worry about during this journey. Things would be ok.

This made the biggest impact on me. You wouldn't believe the comfort that extra t-shirt brought me in knowing that God takes care of the details. I have a quote I wrote on a vase that states "But flowers feed our souls in a different way. They remind us of a God who creates beautiful things and takes notice of the tiniest details." Tricia Goyer. Jesus said "Look at the birds of the air; they do not sow or reap or store away in barns, and yet your Heavenly Father feeds them. Are you not much more valuable than they?" Matthew 6:26 How has God shown you that He cares about the small things? Can you feel the soul quenching love and peace that brings with it? What's a detail God uses to remind you He's there, in control, seated on His throne looking down on you with all His power and authority. For me, it was a t-shirt.

SEPTEMBER 23

> **Rachel Dawn Punneo**
> Sep 23, 2020
>
> Last week I had a fun little trip to the ER where they found a 10-11cm mass on my right ovary. I was able to get in to my new gynecological oncologist today and we scheduled surgery for October 5. If you would please pray for Dr. Gunderson and her team to have the knowledge to identify what this mass is and be able to thoroughly take it out, steady hands to be precise in removing this, and clearheaded to be able to focus on the task at hand. Please pray that she has low stress in the coming weeks, she stays happy and healthy, and is more passionate than ever about her job and her patients.
>
> There are 3 options during surgery:
> 1) It's benign and she takes the right ovary only and zips me back up.
> 2) It's pre cancerous and she'll give me a full hysterectomy and only close observation is necessary.
> 3) It's cancerous. Everything will come out and we'll form a plan then.
>
> She's leaning towards option number 2. If you would also pray for option 1 or 2, I'd appreciate it. If you need more to pray for, let me know. The list goes on with Chris, Luke, Alexis, my mom and sister, school and the people taking my load there, my students, and so on.
>
> God hears prayers and I would absolutely be honored if you lifted a few up on my behalf. Thanks!
>
> 80   109 Comments

Mom and I went to my appointment to meet Dr. Jackson. We talked. I got an exam, an ultrasound, a rectal probe which was a big surprise, and a plan of attack. The good news was that IT WAS STILL THERE! My heart was happy. We scheduled surgery, asked lots more questions, and felt good about moving forward.

I sent this out and the outpouring of love and support was unmatched by anything I've ever felt. I highly recommend pulling a stunt like this, so you know your place in this world and the impact you've made. People are wonderful. In life I've tried to surround myself with upstanding people to fill my village and this just proved how amazing my little village really is. You wouldn't believe the presents and care packs that started flooding in. Ty sent me the book Beautiful Cancer that really helped him. Shelley sent a chemo care pack with toothpaste, t-shirts, BioTene, and more. Church sent a care pack. 4th grade sent an amazing pack with gift cards. Kathy and JoAnn sent the most thorough spot-on care pack with a Friends puzzle, gift cards, snacks, the most voluptuous bathrobe ever, activity books, and so much more. It was amazing! The care and compassion of people is so humbling and comforting. There were constant messages sent, gifts dropped off on the porch, and love felt.

SEPTEMBER 24

It's our 21st anniversary! For the first time in a long time, I was planning on going out, so I got a new dress. We ended up staying in since surgery was on the books now and contracting COVID would make it an instant no go. We celebrated in style at home though. Chris got me an amazing Precious Moments of the back patio and I got a new wedding ring when he proposed to me, asking for another 21 years of marriage together. It's beautiful! *Flashback* I stole his thunder a little bit when we first got married. I called him at work and asked if he could get off work next Friday because I scheduled us an appointment to get married. It wasn't exactly my most romantic moment. Chris called later that day and asked if I was serious. I was. He ended up having to work a half day anyway, but these high school sweethearts ended up getting married and it has lasted this long. After 21 years he got that proposal he always wanted and felt I deserved. It was an action-packed couple of days that were honestly full of joy.

SEPTEMBER 25

A friend of Mom's from Dippin' Dots sent me a prayer blanket with ice cream cones on it from his church. I'm not entirely sure why, but I really liked it. It was nice to know someone prayed for my healing and I could literally and tangibly cover up with it whenever I wanted. Plenty of blankets came in from friends in the coming days, but this was extra special.

The next days were full of waiting, being somewhat careful of moving this mass around too much causing it to hurt again and keeping away from COVID. Easy enough!

SEPTEMBER 29

Blessings are never far when you're in my family. Alexis was always so good about sharing the puppies with me and today was a day she surprised me with a Pollo and coffee day. It was just what the doctor ordered. I had to cancel my hair appointment which I was bummed about BUT, my mom had other plans of course. She contacted Ami, our hairdresser, and got all the materials and directions to color my hair at home with a personalized kit. Ami had perfectly portioned ingredients, directions, notes, tools, and instructions to call if we needed any help. I think Mom has a side hustle if she needs one with this hair gig. The picture of mom adding color to my hair cracks me up. It reminds me of the strung-out chicken meme trying to make it through the week. Lol, I have the best mom for sure.

OCTOBER 1

This was Chris's first official day as Area Manager. This afforded us lots of much needed flexibility during this time. He was able to work from home and take care of me. He would just look at me as I rested in bed at times completely content and comforted by the fact I had the ability to rest at home and do nothing but focus on healing. What an amazing blessing this was!

OCTOBER 4

Surgery prep began with special shower procedures, packing for the hospital, and other little things. Most importantly was begging for prayers though. God's goodness and others bringing me to Him on my behalf was what was going to get me through this.

I named my mass kind of. I had three names for it depending on what it was. If it was benign, her name was Tallulah. If she was precancerous, she was Prancer. If cancer was the outcome, she was Helga. I was ready to meet who was inside me.

> 2:58
>
> **Rachel Dawn Punneo** is with **Chris Punneo** and 2 others.
> Oct 4, 2020
>
> Looking forward to almost all the things that October will bring this year! 😊 As I'm getting ready for surgery and then a 3-5 day hospital stay, I want to thank you for all the support I've felt and prayers said on my behalf. I know I don't even know about all of them. You guys are amazing and I feel your support and prayers.
>
> As you wake up, please start praying again. Chris and I have to be at the hospital no later than 5. Surgery is at 7:30. Please pray for him and encourage him. He will be stuck in the parking lot for hours on end waiting until I get a room.
>
> Also, pray for my mom and sister. The 3 of these people made a promise to protect me a long long time ago and they all have sacrificed much to make sure I was always safe and taken care of. This is a helpless situation for them especially and they need peace tomorrow. Add Luke and Alexis to get an extra dose of peace as well. Pray for Dr. Gunderson, her staff, her hands, her knowledge, her ability to problem solve and identify what's going on. I can't wait to tell you good news tomorrow! Well, Chris is in charge of my fb updates tomorrow... while we're in a praying mood, pray he doesn't tell too many of my secrets while he has power over my fb. 😬 Whew! You might want to set your alarm a little earlier in the morning! 😊 Thank you all!

OCTOBER 5

Surgery day came. It was a big day to be able to rid this mass of my body, no matter who it ended up being. Chris had me to the hospital by 5. He couldn't come in. I had to walk myself in and wait alone. Chris was banished to the parking lot. The thing I hated most about this surgery were the two facts that I couldn't be there to comfort/say I told you so to my family during surgery when they found out the outcome and I couldn't see my kids for the week. One of these things was solved though somewhat. My friend, Lisa, was texting me and she came up with an idea the day before surgery. I would make a video to send to her that she would send to Chris during surgery. That way I could tell him to relax a bit. This made me happy. Between packing a car goody bag for him with snacks and sending these videos I did have some comfort for him that day. He also was able to sign up for text messages that the surgical team would send him.

It's a surreal thing to walk into a building of strangers by yourself, allowing them to drug you, cut you open, and take out your body parts, but that was the plan. I walked in wearing my sister's "Not Today, Satan!" shirt as support and did what they told me from there. It takes an incredible amount of people to get you ready for a surgery. I asked several people who had introduced themselves to me as someone who would be working on me in surgery if they would take pictures of the mass so I could see it. They said they would. When the time came after the changing, cleaning, IVs, directions, last minute questions, and other necessities, it was time for me to walk into the room and lay on the table. I looked around that room knowing God sent his angels to watch over me in there as the doctors worked. They said they wanted me to breathe in the oxygen they were putting on me. They lied. That was the good stuff and the last I recall before waking up in recovery. I remember looking at the clock on the wall trying to figure out the time as I was groggily coming out of sedation. I knew if all had gone well it would have only been a few hours. If it were bad, several more hours would've gone by. I couldn't make it out and couldn't really talk so I just laid there resting. I heard the nurse beside me talking and saying she would update Chris. As I came in and out I kept checking the clock to tell me if I had cancer or not. Eventually, I could feel the meds slowly wearing off in a wave and came to a little more. They moved me up to the 7th floor where I met Chris, my nurse. I asked him if my Chris could come see me now. Pretty soon Chris was able to be there, and I felt so much better to have him by my side, but also nervous for him to tell me what happened and how many parts I had left. I was proud of him when he said, "Well, we got all good news today." He told me they weren't sure what it was exactly they took out because the initial results were inconclusive, but they got it all in one piece. It was completely removed. It didn't look like anything had spread from what they could tell. They did give me a full hysterectomy because they weren't sure what they were dealing with so, per my wishes, they went aggressive right back and took everything out to be safe.

I still didn't know who was in me, Tallulah, Prancer, or Helga. I'd have to wait a week until the final pathology results came back. I wanted to see the picture of what it was, but I'd have to wait. Chris was with me from that point on and that's really what mattered.

That night brought blessings of coming out of/off the heavy meds, minimal movement, trying to FaceTime the kids, Mom, and Kort, and updating people. I also began to love Chris and Mel, my two nurses. Chris was my daytime nurse the first several days and Mel was my nighttime nurse the first several nights. They were fantastic and another blessing to add to the long list.

This smile was the most I could muster. I joked they gave me some Botox with the meds because my face wasn't moving like it used to. Lol. Physical goals tonight included coming off meds without incident, holding down something to eat, pain management, getting up to go to the bathroom by 4:00am, and walking. The first thing I had to eat was a popsicle. Yum! It was delicious. I had a smorgasbord of Elfin crackers and orange sherbet as well. Life was good.

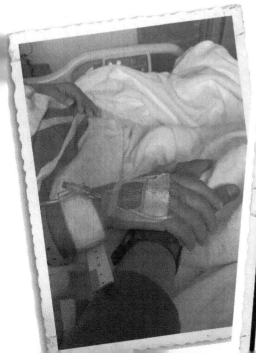

OCTOBER 6

    4am came and I had to make it to the bathroom since they removed my cath. I managed to walk as well since I was already up. Getting out of bed was a Herculean effort that certainly was not without pain, so I tried to maximize the efficiency of my time out of bed. It took all I had to get up and down, but Chris was there every time. I was happy to be back in bed until next time.

    Although my first walking video is boring, we had a hilarious/painfully stupid moment afterwards. I walked into my room after a great walk and thought I'd show off by doing the best Connor McGregor stride ever. It was epic, but bending backwards even a little bit just about killed me. I immediately regretted it, but it was totally worth it! Too bad that wasn't on video.

    As I started the next day, I was looking forward to getting some rehabilitative sleep. Hospital sleep is ironic for the fact they tell you to get good sleep, but they wake you up every four hours for vitals, every time you need meds, when they need to check on you, when a doctor visits, when they clean your room, to survey you about the food, and on and on. This morning was the worst. No joke, every 15 minutes someone came in. Some were welcome visits such as Dr. Jackson. She came in to tell us about surgery finally! She said that the mass had started to attach itself to my intestines, but that she was able to carefully remove it without incident. That was news to us, and another wave of thankfulness came over us that we caught it when we did. This thing meant business.

    Everything went as well as could be expected. I asked to see the picture of it, and no one took one. Ugh, devastation. I wanted to be able to see what had grown inside me and caused all this. No such luck. I guess they were busy saving my life or something. I was disappointed about that for sure, but I had bigger things to tackle in the coming days. Getting up being the monster of them all. I hated it every time, but every few hours I had to. Chris was there with me most of the time, but he did have to make it to some stores throughout the week. I did my job, but no more Connor McGregor impersonations afterwards. I saw what cockiness got me. ;)

OCTOBER 7

Slowly I came off the good stuff and was able to take just Tylenol. Chris and Mel were huge cheerleaders telling me how great and strong I was. They admitted I was their best patient on the floor and that I'd probably be out in record time. They were so encouraging. One nurse was able to get Alexis in on a day when Chris couldn't be there. I think he just wanted to convince her to continue with her degrees and become a nurse. I was ok with that ulterior motive. It was a win-win for me. My walks were getting stronger, longer, and without a pole to rely on. Every time was a struggle, but well worth it. The walls had lots of quotes on them, many from Dr. Suess. Mrs. Valerie told me now that I had surgery, the kids expected me back in a day or two. Ha, NOT that strong yet!

On Wednesday the ladies came in to clean my room. As soon as one walked in I knew immediately even though she was wearing a mask that she was Eraca, one of my 4th graders from Greenvale. I asked her if she went to Greenvale in the 4th grade and she said yes. It was then she screamed "Mrs. Punneo!", ran to my side, knelt, grabbed my hand, and instantly started crying. We talked for a while about us both. I learned she's had a very tough go of things in life, but is working to make a better life for her and her daughter. She prayed an amazing prayer over me before she left and kissed my hand. What a precious soul I was blessed with to encounter during a time no visitors were allowed. I decided then I wanted to do something for her and the children she was charged with taking care of. I called mom up and asked if she wanted to be in charge of a special project. Of course, her answer was yes. She is a girl who loves projects. I decided on a snack basket. She shopped and delivered a basket of great proportions. She even added some cash to help her out in addition to the bounty of snack items. Alexis brought it with her the next day. It was nice to be able to be a blessing when so many were blessing me.

Dr. Jackson came by, and we got the first look at my scar and how it was healing. All were pleased, but Chris the nurse. He said it was a baby scar compared to his. He thought it would've been much bigger and was disappointed. Ha!

OCTOBER 8

I was busting out of this place! Chris and Mel had days off, so it was the perfect time to leave. I didn't want any other nurses taking care of me. Mel won the bet they had going of when I'd be out. I had most of the wires taken out of me, but everything officially came out today and it was the best feeling to not be hooked up to all the things. Every time something came out, it was a huge relief and incredibly freeing. We also set the appointment before I left to see Dr. Jackson for the results from pathology. October 14, I'd go find out the name of the mass that was inside of me.

As I was getting in the wheelchair to leave the hospital, I sat back, and the arm handle went up causing me to fall back. Talk about searing, excruciating pain! It was like a hot knife just stabbed my sutures. I thought I busted all my seams. We stopped, checked as the poor guy driving me looked away, and saw nothing so we continued. Alexis drew the short stick and drove me home while I held on to a pillow between me and the seat belt for live's sake. Alana from school gave me the pillow trick and I'm so thankful she did, and Luke gave me his pillow from Guatemala. It was a brutal ride, but would've been much worse without it. Mom was already at the house waiting on us. We picked up Chick-Fil-A and ate. Then, it was straight to the shower where Alexis helped a

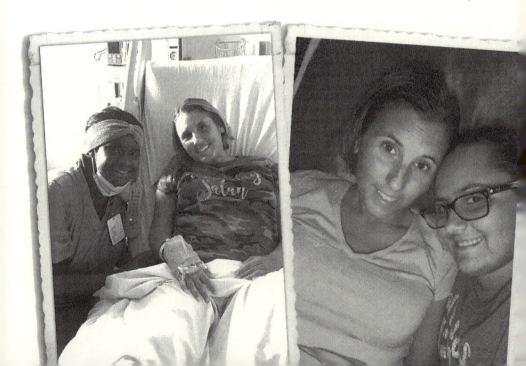

bunch and was pretty much as wet as I was when we were through. She is such a blessing in these instances! I was still girdled up and super bloated, but I was clean, free from wires and machines, and in my own house and that was enough for me to be happy as a fat kid eating cake! The second picture here is when I first climbed into bed. Ahhh! I needed a great deal of help every time I had to get in or out of bed, so I stayed there most of the time just relaxing and recuperating. Somehow my nursing crew improved when I got home. I had the best care in the world hands down. Gifts came pouring in again.

I swear I have the best people around. Amber and Caleb sent me a bag with goodies in it. My sweet friend, Amber, sent me a ton of watercolor supplies. Kort sent flowers in a very special custom picture vase. Armona sent a warm snuggly care pack with a blanket and socks.

OCTOBER 10

Saturday was a big day for me. I got out and spent the day in the living room. It seems small, but I felt like a real human again to be able to enjoy that space. The boys cleaned the house, made the meals, and tended to my every need. I got top notch TLC. The kids even surprised me with a Build-A-Bear sloth they named Flash. They put their voices in him saying, "We love you, Mom" too! He became my piece of them whenever I ventured somewhere with an IV pole. That is his natural habitat. Alexis also brought the wieners over for a bit. Apollo had been to the vet and needed love as much as I did. They always cheer me up. The boys watched Dirty Dancing and Ghost with me. Chris even danced with me through the last and best scene of Dirty Dancing. No lift happened that night! That night as I was getting into bed, I had that searing blast of pain again like when I left the hospital. I checked my stitches and it seemed ok, but I was really worried I did something wrong and did damage.

OCTOBER 11

Mom brought over fresh french toast and I cried a bit telling them I thought I set myself back with that pain the night before. I was mad at myself to let that happen, but sure enough, Mom's french toast made me feel better.

In the days that followed, I was never left alone. Alexis and I started the show "Switched at Birth" and watched a lot of it. The kids competed for best foot rubber - much to my chagrin! ;)

OCTOBER 14

Today is the day I find out who was in me: Tallulah, Prancer, or Helga. I felt awful because today was also the day Luke was scheduled for a small oral surgery. I couldn't be there for him, and I was having mom guilt. In fact, Alexis had to call me from their office because they weren't going to proceed without me there. I had to talk them into it and give verbal permission. It was a close call, but they did it. Ugh, that was stress I didn't need in the waiting room. I already saw a woman crying while waiting to go in. I imagine that's not all uncommon in this waiting room. We waited much longer than normal. Kortney was on FaceTime. Finally, Dr. Jackson came in and checked my stitches and my progress. All was going well. Then, she got to the pathology report. Meet Helga. She was an aggressive little biddy that also surprised her by being in the left ovary a little as well. Seeing that it was ovarian cancer, she was really happy I chose to take everything out when I did. I was diagnosed with stage 1B, high grade serous. Because this cancer was very aggressive, she was going to put me on a 6 round chemo treatment scheduled through March/April. This way if there was something small that was left and growing, we would take care of it, kind of a scorched Earth approach, but I was game. The chance that it would come back without chemo was 50-60%, with chemo it drops to a 20% recurrence. She outlined the treatment plan of 6 rounds three weeks apart starting in a couple weeks to let me rest up from surgery and left so the chemo expert could come in and talk to us next. In between the two I called Amy to tell her. I wanted to let her know I'd be out for a much longer time than expected. I tried to get it out, but yet again with her, the tears came, and I blubbered my way through "I have ovarian cancer and I have to do chemo until April." Mom was there rubbing my back as I talked, and I felt bad I lost it on both of them. In my defense, I'd only dealt with it and processed it for about 10 minutes before then. That's a reasonable excuse, right? Anyways, I laid THAT blubbering mess on her lap and let her finish her day. Then, I went on to talk to all the others about my diagnosis. The chemo expert came in and explained all things chemo. The very first thing she said was, "I can guarantee you; you will lose your hair. This is about all I can guarantee, but I do guarantee that." Well, ok. Let the games begin.

She talked for a long time. Then, we went to another room and talked to the dietician, did a genetic test, took lab work for it, filled out paperwork, and asked more questions. Chris called while I was there. It had taken a while, so he was getting nervous. I didn't want to tell him over the phone, but I had to. He was stuck at home in training and couldn't get out of it. I don't think he took it very well. In fact, he told me later he didn't. You can't blame a guy for that though. I finished up with the genetic testing lab work and was able to leave finally, my head overwhelmed by all the facts, data, and enormity of the situation, but I was ok with this. It was not what I would've chosen, but I knew God needed it to be part of my journey. I'm not sure of the why, but I trusted Him whole-heartedly from the beginning of all this and I wasn't about to stop now. During the appointment she said the vast majority of ovarian cancer is caught either in late stage 3 or usually stage 4. What an unbelievable blessing we were granted by having these 4 episodes of intense pain that could not be ignored. God was not going to allow me to get that far. He said, "Here, take this 2x4! Across the baby maker! Four times!"

We stopped by Braum's because I really wanted a chocolate shake and brought food home for everyone here. Here's to a big stress-free shake - I was not worried about the number of calories that thing had in the moment. I just drank and it was wonderful. This is not a small blessing! The kids were done with surgery by this point and were waiting for Mom and me to get home. I had to tell them the news that no kid ever wants to hear, but we did it together and we were

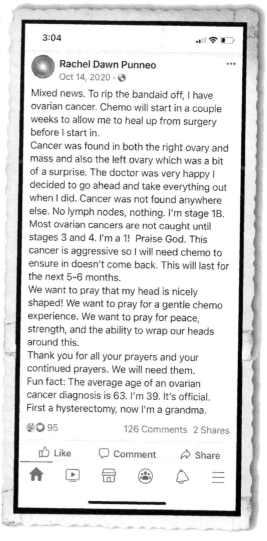

still a family at the end of the day. Also, Luke's surgery went well so we had that going for us. Plus, we got to watch him come off some good drugs, so things were going well for the Punneos.

As always, I Facebooked the news once we let family know. I've said it before. I'll say it again. People are amazing and the best part of this experience. Messages of encouragement came from everywhere and, again, my fourth-grade team at school took on another hard chunk of my work without batting an eye. Within 24 hours, I think Mom and Kort both had teal nails with ribbons and teal outfits. We started on a shirt idea. Luke brainstormed a great "Rachel's Rapscallions" design and made it for himself. Luke and Chris conspired and painted some of my pumpkin's teal. A party was planned to shave my head on the 7th. We were all in on this fight. I had an army behind me ready to take on this battle with me. I love people.

> IN MY BONES, I KNEW THIS WAS BIGGER THAN ME FROM THE BEGINNING. I KNEW GOD HAD SOMETHING HE WAS USING THIS FOR. THERE WAS A PURPOSE, A PLAN, AND I WAS JUST A VESSEL FOR IT. BILL, MY MOM'S HUSBAND, TOLD ME FROM THE BEGINNING OF THIS JOURNEY AS WELL, SOMETHING IS GOING ON HERE. THIS WILL BE USED FOR A GREATER GOOD. PROVERBS 16:4 SAYS, "THE LORD WORKS OUT EVERYTHING TO ITS PROPER END." I WAS BLESSED TO BE ABLE TO FEEL THIS FROM THE FIRST. "THEY WILL HAVE NO FEAR OF BAD NEWS; THEIR HEARTS ARE STEADFAST, TRUSTING IN THE LORD." PSALM 112:7 WHAT IS GOD USING IN YOUR LIFE FOR A GREATER GOOD? ARE YOU OPEN TO BE A VESSEL FOR HIS PURPOSE? IF YOU ARE ALSO ON A CANCER JOURNEY, HOW CAN YOU USE IT TO BETTER OTHERS? I BET IT WILL HELP YOU IN RETURN.

OCTOBER 17

    I was handed a prescription for a cranial prosthesis at my appointment so that meant it was wig shopping day! You can tell from the photo I wasn't exactly into it. I would've loved to have Kort, Mom, maybe some friends come and have a fun party trying on wigs with wine and snacks, but stupid COVID robbed me of that experience. Chris is a trooper though and took me to several places. I decided maybe wigs weren't for me, but I did get the blonde one with the hat. I could pull that one off easy enough and no styling! I'm just hoping and praying my head is nicely shaped enough that I can get away with going bald. Serious prayers were said on behalf of my head! I think my plan is to rock a bald look until it gets weird and funky growing out. Then I may try some wigs during the awkward stages.

    At some point during this time, I talked with Amy again. I did apologize on the night of the 14th about breaking down on her TWICE this year. I'm not sure how she's become the person I go to, to cry, but that seems to be the deal. We talked again about my job. I was worried I'd lose my job somehow getting a new long term sub. Valerie was one of the best blessings ever, but she didn't sign up for 6 months. We had to hire someone else who was more long term given this new news. Amy was quick to assure me I would have a job whenever I was ready. They would be more than ready to have me back. She asked if I wanted to come back on and off and teach on good days. I told her no because I wouldn't be as effective. It'd be a mess to coordinate with another person day to day. The kids would get gypped being in flux between two people constantly. I wouldn't be able to recuperate as effectively if I was stressed about teaching, keeping me out longer potentially in the long run. I didn't think it would be in favor of anyone involved. She immediately answered with, "Good! I think so too! Not that we don't want you back, but we don't want you back until you're 100% and you've taken care of you." I love her and my school beyond belief. They are the biggest blessing. My job is hard. This year it's next level hard. I am blessed with people who say your well-being is so much more important than the toughest thing we can do times 2 for you. I love them and their sacrifices. I never would've thought I would be able to completely leave school behind and not think about taking care of that huge aspect of my life. God has certainly trained me well through the course of 2020 to let go of that control. If this hadn't happened this year, I'm not sure I would've been able to handle giving up my class so well.

Also, Amy asked if it would be okay if the school made a committee to help with anything and everything I could possibly need or want. If I needed someone to pick up groceries, wanted a food pick up, or had a craving for chocolate, they'd be there. It was a real committee with real positions and procedures. I couldn't love this more. I must admit I just didn't want to be forgotten. I told her even if I never used it, it does my heart so much good that I have my own committee! This was next level support! My sister also surprised me by saying she was, without a doubt, she had made up her mind and I couldn't do anything to change it SHAVING her head with me at my party. Are you kidding me?? I have no reasons to ever doubt the goodness of people. She is crazy, but that's why I love her! She's crazy about me.

When all this started, my boys' lives changed overnight, and they became the caretakers of me. They did laundry, dishes, grocery shopping, cooking, anything needed the moment I needed it. They never once complained and don't get all the credit they deserve. Emotionally, I think the caretakers have it worse than the patient many times. All I ever felt was love and peace.

OCTOBER 20

Chris got a hold of Caylan, my nephew, and he got in touch with me when he found out what I was going through. In true Caylan fashion, he sent me lots of reading material. He came by to give me big hugs too. It really was the sweetest thing that he wanted to take care of me in his own way. He passionately gave us lots of information. This is definitely his love language, and I felt his love running deep. He is such a sweet boy and I love him.

OCTOBER 24

As the boys were taking me on a walk, we had some special visitors come BOO us. In our community you can send a POM team member to decorate your front yard in Halloween decor. As we walked around the corner of the house, the Forths were in our front yard! I had two of their kids when they were in fourth grade and the mom was the best volunteer at school ever. I love this family. What a fantastic surprise! They didn't know whose house they were at either, so it was great for both sides. We were able to talk and share in a sweet moment outside that neither one of us expected but probably needed. The Hensleys, who ordered our yard to be booed, blessed us with the decorations and the fellowship!

OCTOBER 27

The last week of October took a definite turn for the worse weather wise. We had an ice storm that completely obliterated the area leaving the roads very icy and so many without power. Like, everybody lost power for days, even weeks. We only ended up losing power for 5 days. On this Tuesday I had an appointment scheduled to get my blood drawn. They told me in no uncertain terms that if I don't get lab work done, I don't get chemo. The roads were bad, but my man got me there carefully and back home safe. Whew! That was a bit stressful. I felt like that was our first obstacle with chemo and it was testing our grit.

Though it fought hard, we fought harder. It doesn't know the moxie of the girl it's dealing with!

OCTOBER 30

To say I was ready to get chemo started may have been an understatement. I convinced Mom to wear a Ghostbusters uniform and go as Cancer Busters. "When there's something strange in your ovaries, who you gonna call? Cancer Busters!" LOL. We had Flash hanging from the IV pole and we were ready to fight. I forgot my new wedding ring so I called up Tamara, my teaching partner, and the head of my committee, and asked if she could swing by the house and bring it to me.

We got the tour from our nurse Dee and cozied up ready for a long day of battle. Really I had no idea what to expect given I'm a complete chemo virgin. IV and pre drugs went in and we were rolling. Dee told me to watch out for back pains and if I felt anything more than I was feeling at that moment she was talking to me, to hit the bell and a whole slew of nurses would drop everything and come running over. We started and life was good...for about 8 minutes. I started to feel some pain low in my butt more so than my back. As I realized it was a thing I told Mom I was going to hit the bell so video the nurses scrambling. She wouldn't. I tried to convince her to for a second, but she wasn't having it and I didn't have time to waste so I hit it. Sure enough, a bunch of nurses jerked their heads in my direction and came running. I pretended to wave a little white flag joking. I was smiling under my mask even. In the few seconds it took her to come over and ask what's wrong and I responded that I felt pain in my butt, she could tell, and I realized I was having a hard time breathing. It was the fastest onset for an asthma attack I've ever felt. She asked if I was having a hard time breathing and things took off so quickly from that point on. I said yes and I knew things were serious at that point. Vitals started urgently and more machines began to be hooked up to me. They said to take my mask off, and I asked if I could take my inhaler. I took multiple hits off that.

    I can't tell you the number of drugs they pushed through my IV, one after another. Nurses kept insisting on pushing so and so amounts of this and that. My mom had been out of the way so the nurses could get in around me. I started drifting in and out, waking up to new people around me each time. Mom later told us my lips were blue and my oxygen dropped to 40. They were about to intubate me. I woke up at one point to check on her and a nurse had her over to the side face to face talking to her. This must have been terrifying for her. I felt better that someone was taking care of her. At one point I woke up to a nurse sticking me with an epi pen. Only, when it hit my leg, I saw a stream squirt past my face. I giggled a little thinking that wasn't supposed to happen. All the nurses stopped, jaws dropped for a second, they scrambled again, then I drifted off again. Next thing I hear was a nurse (later I found out it was Dee) screaming "This is going to hurt!" I woke up for a second before I was stabbed Psycho style in the leg where she then ground it in for good measure. She was right. Apparently, I tried to get up Frankenstein style from the pain. I'm not sure if I kept passing out from the Benadryl, concoction of other drugs, or just not being able to function properly, but I had a couple dreams/hallucinations while I was out. The one I kind of remember was something about Amy and a journal. I woke up after that to see some nice-looking paramedics around me with a stretcher. That was a nice surprise. I remember thinking "Was I just dreaming??" I recalled Amy and the journal and knew funny things were going on if I legitimately had a dream through all that. Not sure if it was sudden onset narcolepsy, just insane amounts of Benadryl, or hallucinations from other drugs, but it was odd. Nurses were still a flurry all around and kept trying to talk to me and get my attention. Eventually I came to enough to get on the stretcher with the help of the paramedics. Maybe I just wanted to impress them. ;) They decided to take me by ambulance 2 blocks down the road to the ER. Mom could meet us there. Picture Mom running through the hospital and parking lot in a Ghostbusters costume cursing at people for the poor design of the ER entrance while calling Chris. That happened. During this whole episode, poor Tamara who made it to my house, called and I'm sure got snipped at by Mom who was watching her daughter slip away. I sure know how to do things up right. In the ambulance, I remember them trying to put in a new IV. My chemo one wouldn't work for what they needed next. They tried at least three times from what I remember in my arms and hands. Then they went to my fingers and tried at least 3 there. No such luck. I remember them asking me for my social and, for the life of me, I couldn't remember. I was really groggy. They gave up on trying to get my SSN and place an IV and gave me to the ER.

I entered the ER and was by myself for a while. A couple more people tried for an IV with no luck. They finally got the head of IVs to come in and do it with the help of a vein ultrasound machine with success! That was good news. I wasn't all the way there, but I knew I was tired of being stuck with needles. One guy came in and did a COVID test on me. I know for a fact I gave him some dirty looks. That was the roughest one I've ever had. I don't know if he thought I was still unconscious or what, but I was not nice with my eyes. Multiple rounds of EKGs ensued. I looked like a toddler who got caught with a sticker book. Stickers were all over me. They took a crazy amount of blood from me, some in vials, some in bottles. I think it was to make room for all the drugs they were adding! The main reason they needed a new IV was because they were sending me for another CT scan which required contrast and a bigger IV to inject it. My chemo IV was too small. Also on the books was an angiogram. Mom was eventually allowed to come in after some cursing and manhandling of the ER attendants I'm sure. Of course, she was cool as a cucumber when she got in front of me. She even took that lovely photo. Nice. Somehow in this mess, I lost my bra, had a blood stain from the EpiPen soaking through my layers of clothes, and looked like an addict. Ha, all in a day's work.

I was wheeled down on my new gurney to get my CT and angiogram done after a while and the CT nurse put the contrast in the wrong IV! I couldn't tell because you must lift your arms over your head. I was still in and out of it a bit and was oblivious which one he put it in. I felt something explode in my right arm and liquid go all over my arm. I looked to my arm and saw the liquid dripping everywhere. I yelled at the CT tech to come over. He stopped, hurried over, and I told him he put it in the wrong IV. Ugh. Add that to the list of things that didn't feel good that day. He corrected his mistake and we tried again successfully. I was wheeled back to the room where Mom was waiting on me. I remember her wanting me to call Kortney. She kept overtly hinting I should FaceTime her. I was trying to make my fingers work and hit the right buttons, but they were not cooperating. Eventually, I yelled at Siri to call her. That didn't work either. I think Mom caught my also overt hint that she should do the calling. I talked to her for a bit, but once I got out "I'm in the ER. Chemo didn't go so great.", I was done.

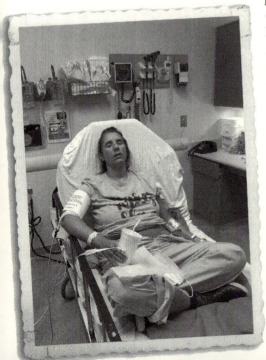

Mom also was communicating with Chris for me. He was on his way up. The results of my tests brought up some things they wanted to monitor so I had to stay in the hospital at least overnight so they could keep an eye on me. Chris was going to come and change the guards at that time bringing me an overnight bag too.

The CT scan showed I had blood clots forming and the EKGs showed I had a blip in my heart. We needed to take measures to fix those before I could leave. We would have never checked for clots or even known we needed to take measures against them without this incident. God was showing the way!

When I got to my room, I kept asking if the nurse would take out my chemo IV. She kept putting me off very nicely, but I kept asking. It hurt and it didn't make sense why I needed it if they had the bigger one in the other arm. I told her about the CT explosion, and she acted as if she didn't believe me or believe that it should be painful. I finally convinced her, and she took it out. Thank God! At that point Chris came in and I just cried on him for a minute. My arm hurt and I think the day caught up with me. I knew I put a lot of people through the wringer today. Tamara! I had a moment of clarity, but no idea if she knew what was going on at that point. I had visions of her still outside my house waiting for me to unlock the house so she could bring me my ring. We called her to let her know what was going on and apologize if Mom snapped at her. Lol, it was a stressful time. Tamara said she made it to my house and called when she got there. Mom answered. Tamara said Mom wasn't rude, but Tamara is also very nice. She said she didn't know what was going on, but that she knew something wasn't right and contacted the committee to start praying and not stop. People. I have the best.

I also called the kids to let them know I was okay. I realized that I would be in the hospital for Halloween, and I wasn't sure when they'd let me out. That was my goal, to get better so I could be out for Halloween. I'd do anything, but I didn't want to miss Halloween with my family. If you know me, that was incomprehensible.

"Though you have made me see troubles, many and bitter, you will restore my life again; from the depths of the earth, you will bring me up." Psalm 71:20 This was a definite low of this journey for me. My life had to be saved. I went from a Ghostbusters costume celebrating fighting to a hospital bed quick, fast, and in a hurry. Your life can seem to go from great to ruins in just minutes sometimes, but Romans 8:28 promises, "We know that in all things God works for the good of those who love Him." God can and will use your lowest, scariest moments to open your eyes, bring you close to Him, and show you, you need Him. Thank God for those times! "We also glory in our sufferings, because we know that suffering produces perseverance; perseverance, character; and character, hope." Romans 5:3-4 Think about those moments in your life. What was the collateral beauty that came from it?

OCTOBER 31

A doctor came in to talk to us, a colleague of Dr. Jackson. He told us that I would continue with the same drug, Taxol, but we would titrate it, so it went in slower. So, I'll just die a slower death?? When I asked what the success rate was of this, he said 99%. I asked what happens when I'm the 1%. We weren't the biggest fans of each other. Especially when I asked him about medical marijuana. That obviously was not his favorite subject. Either way, he said if I took IVs of some potassium and magnesium, finished my blood thinners, and my EKG came back better, I could leave today. Sign me up!

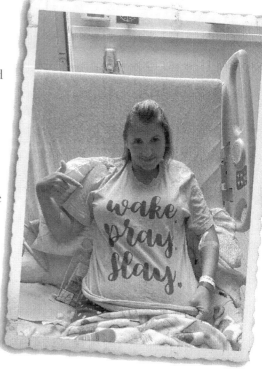

We got home around 2:00 that day. We told everybody we'd host Halloween if we got home, and the power was on. We still didn't have power when we got home, but the Fonzis brought over a generator we could use. At this time, this was the epitome of all gifts. Nobody had power and everybody was out of them so there was no hope of buying one. We were able to power the tv for the game, the refrigerator, and the heat. We used candles for light, stepped over extension cords, and made Halloween happen like normal...you know, if normal was straight out of the hospital, during a pandemic, with no power, hiking through fallen tree branches. I couldn't have been happier. Our whole family came together and had one of the best Halloweens to date even if it was thrown together in a few hours. Tradition prevails! Also, Heather came by and surprised us with a goody basket full of movies, breads, and candy. My heart could've burst thinking about waking up in the hospital and looking at where we were now. There was one thing though. Chris had been having some pains on his left side and high blood pressure he began to worry about. Mom was the one who finally convinced him to go to the ER. I love her. After everyone left, we went back up to the ER and Hospital that started our whole cancer journey. They wouldn't let me in at all by this point. Chris had to go in by himself and make sure he wasn't having/had/or is in danger of having a heart attack. He gave them a handful of trouble because he had to get an IV which he wasn't a fan of. I was in the parking lot late on Halloween night by myself which is super scary to me. While waiting in the parking lot, Clay, our pastor, happened to check in on me. What a blessing! Even though Chris didn't want to let a lot of people know, I told Clay to pray for us and this situation. Knowing that there was prayer for us made the waiting more bearable. God's timing is unbelievable at times. For Clay to check in on us at that exact moment was surely divine. This was one more scary situation that God was able to take care of for us proving His goodness- as if we needed more proof. Chris passed with flying colors! That relieved a lot of stress in itself. After a very long day that started and ended with hospital visits, we were headed home, albeit a home without much power, but it is our home which we loved.

NOVEMBER 1

While Saturday was full of crazy energy (I think I had lots of steroids among the drugs) and just the joy of Halloween, Sunday I crashed. I slept a good chunk of the day. TMI alert: I had my first intense battle with constipation. We won't speak of the details I endured with that. My cheeks were still red. In fact, yesterday my mother-in-law thought I put on some bold makeup for my costume, lol. We all desperately needed rest that day and we got it as well as the power coming back on! This was a good day for sure. We needed some normal and we were so happy to get it. Although it did show how messy our house had become in the past week! It was certainly an action-packed week if nothing else!

NOVEMBER 4

Dr. Jackson obviously wanted to see me to discuss what happened Friday. She explained that I went into a very rare, very severe anaphylactic shock due to the Taxol. Because of this, she didn't want me to continue using this, not even slower. I cannot tell you how relieved I was to hear this news. The doctor in the hospital said we'd continue, and I was so nervous about going through that again. Dr. Jackson is a Godsend. She is right on with our ideals and intensity to fight this. She assured me Taxotere is still very effective. We wouldn't be settling with this drug. I also asked if we could titrate the new Taxotere just to be safe. We could always speed it up later, but we needed a win starting up again. She agreed and I was so thankful she let me make that call. We absolutely love her and how she listens to what I need even if it's not the typical way of doing things. I also asked her about medical marijuana, and she was very sympathetic explaining that a lot of patients find relief from symptoms with it and could be used if needed. She didn't make me feel stupid, inferior, or like a feigning crackhead. She was sympathetic and real with an awkward conversation. The next step was waiting for insurance to approve the new drug and then I would have the first seat in chemo again.

NOVEMBER 7

This was supposed to be the day of my hair shaving party. I postponed it until I had a successful chemo treatment. I wasn't about wasting weeks bald when I didn't have to. Kortney was planning on coming down anyway, so we decided to save the date and just make it a cookout. This was the first time I'd seen her since all this started and it was such a treat! Tamara and she had been in cahoots planning a surprise parade for me. Tamara invited my current classes and the staff. Some people from the church even came! They brought posters, flowers, and gifts, but still kept their distance! It was a really fun day; one I won't quickly forget.

They also gifted me some pretty cool gifts including a rainbow unicorn hat and this bracelet from school that reads "Beautiful girl, you can do hard things." I made sure to wear it to every chemo treatment. I really do have the best people. Even in hard times, there's so much collateral beauty. I'm so thankful God has blessed me with a village that cares, shows support, and acts. These kids that showed up only knew me for a few weeks through zoom lessons. I was not a wonderful teacher. This came from the goodness of their hearts, not any steadfast rapport we had. I'm telling you; great people are all around when you look.

Love these People

NOVEMBER 9

I had to go to OU again to sign some papers for the new meds. The nurse just came out to the waiting room, and we took care of it there quickly. This is where I learned Dr. Gunderson was becoming Dr. Jackson and that Taxotere often has much more mild side effects than Taxol. Woohoo! I was happy to take that on.

NOVEMBER 11

Alexis came over to watch some "Switched at Birth". I called to check on the insurance because I knew our window was closing for me to be able to get chemo in this week. I was so happy when they said we were a go for chemo. Alexis and I ran out to get the bloodwork taken care of immediately. We went to OU so that there was minimal wait time for them to get the results.

True, I was very excited to get on the road to recovery, but it wasn't lost on me that they had to save my life last time and I was heading into the fiery furnace again. Since all this started, Kortney has always brought up one of my favorite Bible stories of Shadrach, Meshach, and Abednego. She always declares, "They came out unsinged without even the smell of smoke on them!" That's me. That's my story. I came out from my first chemo experience, a very scary moment, unsinged. I'm no worse for wear. I had my angel walking there with me keeping me safe

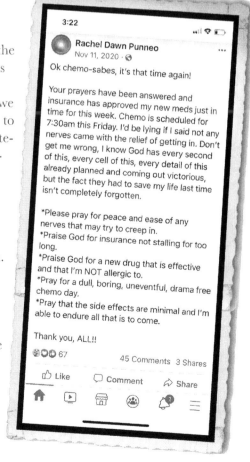

Rachel Dawn Punneo
Nov 11, 2020

Ok chemo-sabes, it's that time again!

Your prayers have been answered and insurance has approved my new meds just in time for this week. Chemo is scheduled for 7:30am this Friday. I'd be lying if I said not any nerves came with the relief of getting in. Don't get me wrong, I know God has every second of this, every cell of this, every detail of this already planned and coming out victorious, but the fact they had to save my life last time isn't completely forgotten.

*Please pray for peace and ease of any nerves that may try to creep in.
*Praise God for insurance not stalling for too long.
*Praise God for a new drug that is effective and that I'm NOT allergic to.
*Pray for a dull, boring, uneventful, drama free chemo day.
*Pray that the side effects are minimal and I'm able to endure all that is to come.

Thank you, ALL!!

from all harm. In fact, we found my blood clots through that experience and potentially saved my life through it inadvertently. Not only did I come out of that fire unsinged and without the stench of smoke, but I smelled better! God is good! Despite the fact that I knew I was going to be ok through it all, I'd be lying if I denied there weren't a little bit of nerves for the upcoming treatment. Enter the prayers of my chemosabes!

NOVEMBER 13

Friday the 13th sounds like the perfect day to tackle this, right? Mom and I walked in again. I made them take Mom in again because I told them my first, first time didn't count. This was my real first time. They didn't argue too much but did tell me absolutely no one could come in after this treatment. That changed a lot of plans. We were going to have Kort, and Alexis come in for some treatments too. We had plans. Ugh, cancer and COVID!

We were set up right at the front spot by the nurse's station. In fact, the chemo floor wasn't open that day. They worked me in as well as a couple other quick patients. I have no idea how that worked out, but I'm sure God had a little something to do with it. I told Chris if they didn't hear my bell, I could throw it at them from where I was. Knowing my aim, he knew I was close! We were blessed with Dee again. She knew my experience. She told us then that the first girl that epi penned me got her thumb too! She also said she was the one who did it the second time. I made sure to show her my bright bruise! After talking with her some about that day, it's funny the impression I made on everyone. Both in the office and at chemo, everyone seems to know exactly who I am and how much I scared them all before. We got started at a titrated pace and passed 8 minutes- that's how long Dee said it was last time. Woo! We made it to the next level, and I started to feel back pain again. It came on quick and strong. I rang my bell and Mom jumped out of the way again. Dee immediately stopped my meds, took my vitals, and let me relax and breathe through these. I was scared, but following directions, and before you know it, I was on the other side of it without much episode or too much worry at all. We continued with treatment, and I didn't have a single problem after that! Thank God! Thank God! Mom and I were so happy walking out of there of my own physical ability on two feet - not on a stretcher headed to the ER. We did it. We had a win under our belt!

Support came from great sock choices, two cute blondes wearing a cute shirt, and Mrs. Valerie on her last day with the kids. I was home in record time that day ready to rest!

In the days following chemo, I had definite mouth

weirdness (as I call it), a super dry nose with lots of blood, constipation, one bout of hair loss, low energy, and some aches, but overall, it wasn't too bad.

Ms. Danielle was named as my temporary long-term sub. She was Luke's and Kayden's student teacher for the beginning of this year in Biology. They both liked her a lot so that made me feel better.

Alexis and I were having fun working with some last-minute hairstyles.

I got to pick up my cookies and I was so happy. She first sent me a picture and my uteri had crowns instead of halos. I was really sad. I asked if she could fix them but realized it would be ok if she couldn't. My uterus was in heaven and had earned its crowns for the work it put in holding and protecting two great kids. She did fix them anyway though. I tried them and they were delicious too!

Last day of bed head!

NOVEMBER 21

The day finally came that I was shaving my head, but I wasn't the only one. So many people decided to support me and shave their heads as well, one being Mom. She, much like her equally stubborn daughter, told me she was shaving her head with me as well. I could not change her mind. It was not my decision. Well, ok then. What do you say to that?? Among the other shavers were Kort, her husband, Wes, my father-in-law, Timmy, and Chris. We were waiting to get started and my stomach was dropping a little. I wanted badly to get this going. I'd had moments of slight anxiety about a bald head in the past weeks, but I figured it was a rite of passage in the cancer club. It was time, but Laci, my sister-in-law, wasn't there yet. They wanted me to wait because Laci would feel bad if she wasn't there. I was about to lose my ever-lovin' mind. I had to move inside and pace so I wouldn't go crazy. Chris had to stop me and hold me for a bit. That helped. Laci finally showed up and we began. Pink played. Clippers were buzzing. Let's do this. Luke shaved my head per his request. I shaved Timmy's head per his request. I was pumped to get started because I was really excited about getting a mohawk. That was the best part of all this. I was rocking a mohawk throughout the party as was everyone else who was shaving. We'd break for lunch then finish finally shaving all the rest off. I'd be the first to get a mohawk and the last to have. Because pictures are worth a thousand words, I'll let them speak for themselves. Know it was the best time ever. Really so much fun!

Luke surprised us and had his sister give him a mohawk. He kept it instead of shaving the whole thing, but that took everyone by surprise. So, we had 7 people total get new dos today! That's unbelievable to me! The love this family has for each other is crazy! After everyone got their mohawk, we relaxed and ate Rib Crib and amazingly cute cookies. I felt so much better at this point. I had my mohawk and I was happy. When we were fat and sassy, we got to shaving again. I was the last to go this time. The whole day was such a big blessing. Many thanks to Bill for capturing so much of it! This day was full of SO. MUCH. LOVE. Collateral beauty really showed today. Once everybody left with a cookie in hand, it was up to Chris and me to finish shaving my head. I'll tell ya, that was the scariest part. We went in the shower, and he took a straight razor (when I was on blood thinners!) to my head. It didn't feel great at all, and I was super nervous, but like all other pieces to this journey, it came out fine and we had a final product. Chris liked it. I liked it. It was my new style! And, as it turns out, my head was shaped nicely! Check one more prayer off the answered prayer list!

"Praise be to God, who has not rejected my prayer or withheld his love from me!" Psalm 66:20 "The Lord has done great things for us, and we are filled with joy." Psalm 126:3 Ecclesiastes 8:15 gives us these refreshing words, "So I commend the enjoyment of life, because there is nothing better for a person under the sun than to eat, and drink, and be glad." Man, sometimes we just need to send God prayers of thankfulness, joy, and praise. We need to shout from the rooftops how good He is to us. This was one of those days. This was a day of deep contentment and joy. I know there are many hard days throughout a cancer fighter's journey, but I also know that there are more good days than bad. Because you know how low the bad days can go, you can appreciate and relish the good days even more. What has been the best day of your journey? Why?

NOVEMBER 24

One thing I asked for Christmas was massages. I heard about all the aches and pains chemo brings on and I thought that would be the perfect thing to help alleviate some of that. Of course, Chris couldn't wait to give me early presents, but this was one time I sure didn't mind. Because he knew I didn't want to get out and go places with COVID around, he even found someone to come to the house. She was cautious about cleaning everything. I was happy.

With each massage I wore my new voluptuous robe Kathy and JoAnn got me. I felt like I was on the bougie cancer treatment plan with my in-home masseuse. My amazing husband also gave me these shirts early, but I needed to start wearing them before Christmas anyway. Receiving early presents is apparently another mindset change 2020 brought. Who knew?

NOVEMBER 25

My hair kept growing in, so Chris had to do some upkeep on it to keep it bald. It's ok, he owes me from shaving his head for so many years now. It got easier each time with better tools, and I eventually started doing it myself in a jiffy.

Today was also the day we got a call from Mom saying she had COVID. She lost her taste and smell, went, and got tested, and sure enough, she was positive. Ugh, it finally happened. It hit our group and one of the ones I was worried about, my 70-year-old mom with Lupus. The next day's Thanksgiving was obviously cancelled. Family from out of town who were staying over there left that day. We went into communication mode for everyone who was at the head shaving. The one get together I throw was now tainted with stupid COVID despite all the precautions we took.

NOVEMBER 26

Thanksgiving was spent with just the 3 of us at our house for the first time ever. We didn't even see Alexis. Luke made some breakfast burritos, and we had an average day here at Punneo's Palace.

NOVEMBER 27

I woke up, blew my nose with a fresh box of my favorite Vicks Kleenex, and could barely smell it. I ate peanut butter waffles with syrup and could only smell the syrup a little, not tasting much of the waffles. I knew I had to get tested and everybody else too. We went to the Family Clinic, and I was positive. Chris was negative. They didn't test Luke. I was so upset. How could I let this happen? Chemo was obviously delayed now. I called OU immediately to let them know and they confirmed, no chemo on the 3rd. My mom's husband and my mother-in-law also tested positive. I felt so responsible because of my party. Now Cherri, my mother-in-law, had it- another one on my "Do Not Let Her Get It" list that I tried so hard to protect. We went home with masks on. I was in the middle of decorating for Christmas, and I couldn't finish now. I didn't want to touch anything. Luke measured out a safe 6 feet from my spot on the bed and I started my quarantine from the boys. It was so hard. I lived in our bedroom and bathroom. Chris stayed on the couch for about a week and then on an airbed Mom delivered in the living room. The boys came in to give me food and would spend limited times with me talking in the safely distanced seat. All interactions were with masks. That day the boys went out to our tree farm and picked it out, cut, put up, and decorated our tree all by themselves. This is not something they necessarily love doing, but they did it for me. I did watch from the hallway with a mask on at one point to feel like I was kind of a part of it. They were amazing!

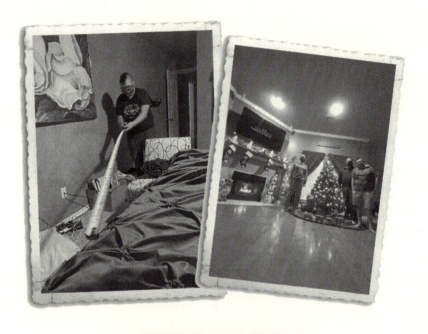

NOVEMBER 29

I never had too hard of a time during COVID symptom wise. My breathing was fine. I felt fine. I just couldn't taste or smell. That was hard in its own right though. I really love food. I found myself eating more to try to irrationally find something I could taste. No comfort food worked. It was like I was never satisfied. Duh, I wasn't. They say repeating something expecting different results is a sign of insanity. Well, they're not far off. Coupled with being stuck in my room

99% of the day, I gained more weight. Weather was cold a lot of days, so walking wasn't always an option, but I did when it was doable. The boys still walked me just with masks and 6 feet away. I did some yoga and light exercise videos in the bedroom because I was worried about inactivity and my clots. It was a fine line between not getting my breathing worked up too much tempting COVID and not moving enough tempting clots and weight gain. I kept myself entertained with "A Million Little Things" and other shows recommended to me that I didn't figure Chris would like. I went to bed when I wanted and did what I wanted which was nice, but I sure missed spending time with my boys. We just couldn't risk getting anyone sick that maybe couldn't handle it and you never knew who that would be.

I still had to finish up the Shutterfly calendars for Christmas and usually do tree pictures for December's page since I really have to finish in November. I asked the boys for pictures and Chris got a little upset that I didn't want to be in it. I didn't want to be too close to them, even masked. He got on to me a bit and I begrudgingly took a quick pic. It certainly wasn't full of the Christmas joy it usually is.

NOVEMBER 30

On Nov. 18 Amy announced that her husband, Todd, had bladder cancer. It did not look good. Come to find out they would also find it in his lungs and become quite the formidable opponent. Amy would call me, and we would talk, or text and I would try to provide any advice and support I could. From the beginning of my experience, I had been taking notes from friends like Regina, Julie, and Kathy who had their own journeys with cancer. You could just tell their support was a little different and a little more special and practical than somebody who had not gone through this type of thing. I knew I'd be able to pay this forward someday, but I didn't know it'd be so soon. Today, Amy called and asked if I was ready to return the favor. I said yes not fully knowing what I was agreeing to, and she just broke down on me like I did on her twice. They received more bad news at the doctor, and she knew things would be incredibly hard and intense, a battle tougher than most. This was not going to be easy. I helped with what I could, mainly just listening. I felt so humbled to be able to be her person at that moment. We've become pretty close through all this, swapping stories and a ton of support each way. More bonded, steadfast, and meaningful relationships have proven to be a side effect worth enduring this.

She also called to tell me she wouldn't be part of a "Rachel's Care Team Committee" sanctioned event today. They were going to surprise me and scheduled a visit so I could have some type of excitement. The plan was to knock on my window by the bed, but since word got out to me (I've been bad about inadvertently ruining surprises by seeing things I shouldn't), I just went to the front door which was a nice trip in itself. I forgot to take pics, but Amy sent me some. Our new library aide even brought by a beautiful handmade blanket!

Danielle, my long-term sub, also started school and posted from my room today. I keep forgetting I redesigned it over the summer and it's weird to think other people are breaking it in for me.

DECEMBER 1

My Uncle Greg sent me a beautiful wig from his daughter Alicia when she battled cancer. It is the most natural, nicest one I have. It really could be worn, and no one would realize it was a wig. I also got to the part in "A Million Little Things" where a character wore her pink wig, and I finally knew who Tawnie was comparing me to. Laci got this pink wig for me, so I had to send a pic of me sporting it with Maggie. My wig collection was growing in positive ways. And it was all due to other people's kindness.

Chris also came in and we had a heart to heart. It was difficult to have such a vulnerable conversation and not be holding each other. Instead, we ended up doing the best we could connecting with our feet as far away as we could. He explained why he got so irritated the other day with me when I just wanted the two of them in the calendar picture. With all that's going on, he hated more than anything for me to be absent in that picture. It symbolized and made real his worst fear at the end of all of this... that I wouldn't be in any more pictures because I wouldn't be there. I got that and understood where he was coming from. Even if that wasn't my fear, I understood this is all very scary to watch from his point of view.

We didn't really tell anybody about my COVID until this post except for those who needed to know and school. I was too upset with myself for having the head shaving party. I did end up feeling better about that though. I realized that everybody who got it would have got it regardless. We were all in each other's inner circle. No one got it on Chris's side, thank God! We didn't spread it there.

I sat in my room for 10 days by myself with COVID. There was only one day where I really became bummed. Don't get me wrong, there were plenty of bad parts to it, the worst being away from my boys and the next being unable to taste. I always try to look for the good and found it even there, but one day I just wasn't feeling it and didn't feel bad for not trying to.

> I WANTED TO GIVE MY HUSBAND A CHANCE TO SHARE A BIT OF HIS SIDE AND ADVICE HERE. I'VE ALWAYS SAID CANCER IS HARDER ON THE CAREGIVERS THAN THE PATIENT IN MANY WAYS. HE VOWED A LONG TIME AGO TO PROTECT ME, AND TO WATCH ME GO THROUGH THIS WAS A HELPLESS SITUATION FOR HIM. HERE ARE HIS THOUGHTS:
>
> ANYONE'S FIRST THOUGHTS WHEN THEY HEAR THE WORD CANCER IS THAT THEY'LL LOSE THEIR LOVED ONE. RACHEL IS NOT JUST MY LOVED ONE. SHE'S MY SOULMATE. AT THIS POINT WE HAD BEEN TOGETHER HALF OUR LIVES. THERE'S NOT A MEMORY I HAVE THAT SHE'S NOT IN. THE THOUGHT OF BEING WITHOUT HER IS UNIMAGINABLE. I KNEW SHE HAD THE MOST UNBELIEVABLE FAITH OF ANY PERSON I'VE EVER MET, AND SHE IS A FIGHTER. EVEN KNOWING ALL OF THAT, I COULDN'T HELP BUT THINK HOW I WOULD GO ON WITHOUT HER. THESE THOUGHTS WERE IN MY HEAD JUST ABOUT EVERY DAY. AFTER SHE WAS DIAGNOSED I SPENT EVERY MINUTE I POSSIBLY COULD WITH HER NOT KNOWING HOW MUCH TIME WE HAD. THEN SHE GOT COVID ON TOP OF THE CANCER WHICH REQUIRED US TO QUARANTINE AWAY FROM EACH OTHER FOR 10 DAYS, THE HARDEST 10 DAYS OF MY LIFE. THIS MADE AN ALREADY DIFFICULT SITUATION THAT MUCH HARDER. THIS SITUATION MADE ME QUESTION MY FAITH QUITE OFTEN BECAUSE I FELT I HAD LIMITED TIME WITH HER, AND TO HAVE TO SEPARATE FOR 10 DAYS GAVE MY MIND TIME TO RUN WITH THOUGHTS OF WHAT IT WOULD BE LIKE WITHOUT HER. I FELT SELFISH WHEN I PRAYED BECAUSE ALL I COULD THINK ABOUT

to pray for was that He didn't take her away from me. I do believe that God has a plan for everything, and it scared me to think that maybe His plan wasn't to have her here anymore. Even though I trust His plan, I didn't believe I was strong enough to go on without her. However, I started to see all the lives she impacted through different areas of her life as love and support poured in from these people during this tough time. Even people we didn't even know reached out to us. I realized then it wasn't God's plan for Him to take her from us, but it was to introduce her to a whole other group of people that fight this nasty disease that we could help. I began to find strength and optimism that God's plan was to shine His light through her to show others that you can put any problem into His hands, and everything will be ok. This has been an amazing journey watching God work through her to help so many people battling cancer. "Let your light shine before men in such a way that they may see your good works and glorify your Father who is in heaven." Matthew 13:43 Caregivers can find solace in 2 Corinthians 1:3-4 "Praise be to the God and Father of our Lord Jesus Christ, the Father of compassion and the God of all comfort, who comforts us in all our troubles, so that we can comfort those in any trouble with the comfort we ourselves receive from God." How has God turned what you felt was a selfish prayer into something for His good?

DECEMBER 7

I hadn't planned on getting tested so quickly because OU told me there can still be false positives causing me to have to wait an additional 20 days for chemo. We were currently scheduled for December 18, but Chris's work needed both Chris and me to have additional negative tests. I figured if I got another positive, I'd just keep it to myself until it was time to test with OU again. Chris and I went to the Family Clinic again when the time had passed according to the CDC and COVID police (aka OK Dept. of Health) who called me during my stint. My 10 days had come and gone, and I was incredibly relieved to get the amazing news that we were both negative. We had managed to not spread it and all that time away was worth it!

I went home with all the energy in the world. I took a shower, stripped every last thing down, did tons of laundry, Clorox and Lysoled everything that couldn't go in the wash, completely disinfected my room (ground zero), put up Chris's bed and washed his sheets, and cleaned every surface. Most importantly I hugged my son and my husband. I'd been waiting for so long to do that safely. It felt good down to the soul. I fessed up to OU saying I got a negative test, and I was ready to test for them as well.

DECEMBER 8

I got an appointment for today with results coming tomorrow. In the meantime, I soaked up all the love and snuggles I could with my boys not in my room, but Chris sure was happy to return. Luke had been taking care of all things Elfie up to this point, but I was taking some of the reins back there too. It felt so good to be a part of things again.

DECEMBER 9

My nurse from OU called and I was in shock, devastated and angry when they said I tested positive again. She also quietly allowed me to keep my chemo appointment for the 18th because my symptoms started enough days ago, I would be in the clear and no longer contagious according to anyone's standards. She did warn me of testing too early and getting a positive. While that was the good news, I was beside myself that I could have potentially gone through everything I did to isolate myself and just infected my boys in the past two days. I was hot. This was the worst mood of the whole journey. Again, I allowed myself the day to be as bitter as I wanted to be, but expected better for the next day. And I was. I couldn't help what happened next or if anyone else got it. It was too late at this point to do anything about it now. It was what it was in this stupid COVID pandemic, and I know I did everything in my power to do what was right and safe according to the people who were supposed to know. I did swear to not make that same mistake twice. Fool me once, shame on COVID. Fool me twice, shame on me. I was going shut in style. I knew I couldn't fight cancer and COVID simultaneously, so I had to do whatever it took to keep away from it.

Throughout December dress up days started at school, and I posted a pic with a bow on my head as a show of solidarity. Amy posted it on Good Morning, Independence, our daily live virtual morning assembly, and it quickly became a thing. Every day I was featured on GMI. Luke got to sift my head with flour for "Top It Off" day. Who needs a hat when your head is 1/3 snowman?! One day I was challenged to make a video for jingle day. It had mixed reviews, so I ecstatically made mean tweet reading video. I wanted to do that forever, lol!

One big blessing from my school was them always reminding me I'm still a part of them and not forgotten.

DECEMBER 11

My heart grew 3 sizes tonight. Some of the best girls ever surprised me with some caroling at my front door. I haven't seen these students' faces since March. I never got to say goodbye then. We didn't know it was the end. I still didn't get within 6 feet, but I promised the biggest squeezes at the end of the year. Who knew how much good this could do a soul?! I shut the door and teared up. I love them an unbelievable amount and couldn't be more honored they thought of me.

DECEMBER 18

Life went on happily and quietly. I joined my two classes on Zoom for their Christmas parties thanks to Tamara's invite. They are a mess and I'm so thankful I'm not tasked with putting up with all that energy and stress daily. It is a true blessing to just be able to focus on nothing but healing and following your body's lead when it tells you to just rest. I've always said this is my early year of retirement since I had to use all my sick days I was planning on turning in for an early year of retirement. I'm trying to make the most of them and not feel guilty for it. Today helped me to realize they're going to a good cause. Those kids are exhausting!

Kortney took me to my next chemo (cycle 2) although she wasn't allowed in. She made the trek all the way down here just to sit in the car for hours and wait for me to take me home. Luke came and spent time with her too in the car. Luckily, she was able to get some last-minute shopping taken care of now that she had the time. One of my three favorite moments of chemo days are Kort's prayers before we start so I was blessed to get her magic in person today before I headed in by myself. In fact, Mrs. Valerie prayed with us too because I was invited to our Christmas party which I was zooming on while loading up. I think seeing everybody from school really got me amped up because I had to wait to get started with chemo until my heart rate went down and my vitals became calmer.

I had a seat at the end of the nurse's station by the back door this time and a new nurse which I was a little bummed about. I thought I'd be able to keep Dee by my side the whole treatment schedule. Chemo went well once we got going. I had to stop because of some back pains. My vision was blurry at one point too. Because no one was with me, Chris, Mom, and Kort wanted me to FaceTime the whole treatment so they could keep an eye on me. It's not the most relaxing way to go about chemo, but it put them at much needed ease, so I obliged. They got to see the stopping, reaction, and everything. It was minor and we started up again soon, so all was well for the first go around by myself. Once again, I was able to walk out of chemo on my own two feet and I felt blessed for it. My other favorite parts of chemo days are walking out to the parking garage and seeing Luke greet me and Tallie and Tawnie's picture in their shirts. I got some extra Kortney woot woots too! Winning!

I'm not sure why or when anything changed with my mental state, but Christmas was coming and COVID was getting more out of control. I'm not sure if I watched too much news, if the new strains breaking out got to me, or what, but I started to stress a lot about what should be the best day of the year. Kortney had plans to come down and spend it with us. I was so happy about it. Maybe memories of how we spread COVID to the Atchison's at Thanksgiving may have incited worry, but I was not at peace with being around others and their bubbles. I know it doesn't quite make sense. I had just seen Kort at chemo, but the worry of having so many around with new bubbles like my nephew's girlfriend was worrisome. It was heartbreaking to tell them though. I felt like I was ruining everything special because no one really knows how this COVID thing works. I wanted to put myself in a bubble, but it's horrible that I affect others when I do so. Kort decided not to come down so I could have a Christmas kind of. She said she was blessed with a normal Thanksgiving, so it was our turn to try to make a normal Christmas. I really do have the best big sister ever. I know this whole process has been so hard on her, and me not being present physically exasperates all the hardest times. It really is the most stressful part of this whole journey. I want more than anything to be with her and share this with her, but I have to also keep myself COVID free because there is no way to fight cancer and COVID at the same time. I tried. To take risks is irresponsible. Kort, of course, understands all this, but it is so hard when you love someone so much. The days leading up to Christmas were a little sad. I was working through chemo days and trying not to focus on disappointing the ones I loved the most.

This bout was not bad. I had mouth weirdness, constipation that turned to diarrhea, blood in my nose and weird boogers, and some aches and pains. Overall, when I was on the other side of it, it was a mild run of side effects.

DECEMBER 22

I was surprised with the best visitors tonight. These 3 kids will always go down as some of the most special humans ever. They took it upon themselves to make me cards (or in Snow's case, a book!) and deliver it to say hi. Are you kidding me?!? I can't even with these guys. What teenage kids do you know that would prioritize their 4th grade teacher's happiness into their lives? We had to FaceTime Brugh, my former teaching partner and their other teacher that year, to let her in on the fun too. This picture is the epitome of collateral beauty. Situations like this allow for the God given beauty inside people's souls to shine through. They left with air hugs and promises for real ones at graduation.

DECEMBER 24

Christmas Eve came and we had a fairly normal time. Like always Cherri, Roger and Alexis came over to spend it together. I'm a little embarrassed to say that I made Alexis take a shower and change into fresh clothes first thing when coming over. I watched everything that was touched like a hawk and disinfected as soon as I could. I Lysoled where everyone sat. I tried to keep my 6 feet away at all times and changed clothes afterwards too. I wasn't comfortable and wasn't my best self while celebrating this year. We figured most of us had it this year and were immune for a while, but I still saw COVID as a risk that I couldn't fully control.

We kept up with the traditions of Elfie and reindeer food. We even watched "Christmas Vacation" with Papa and some other Christmas cartoons. Grinch drinks were made as well.

DECEMBER 25

The dogs and kids were all home and ready for Christmas. We did our normal morning which was wonderful. Alexis gave me quite the present. She is the most compassionate, kindhearted girl. She collected notes of encouragement from people in all areas of my life and presented me with a journal of these precious thoughts to get me through tough times. This journal stays in my chemo bag.

Instead of going to my mother in laws to celebrate like we would traditionally do, we FaceTimed Christmas in with Sally, Timmy, Laci, Rhett, Tawnie, Josh, and Tallie, opening presents that Alexis had delivered earlier in the week to each side. I even let the presents sit to decontaminate before we opened them.

We did head over to Mom's and of course I was a little antsy. I tried to steer clear even though they both had COVID earlier when I did. We only stayed for presents and dinner to keep it short, but man it was delicious. Mom made a traditional Thanksgiving meal, and it was everything! It wasn't my finest state of mind there either though. I failed with a disheartened approach to what should have been Christmas magic. In the end, we had love and we were all safe afterwards. I was ready to go home, bubble up and not have to worry about gatherings anymore even if it was with the people I loved. I was ready to finish chemo, finish cancer, and focus on getting back to a real normal.

When I got home I tried to sign up for an empowerment shoot through Tenaciously Teal. They do these for cancer patients, and it made me happy to think of scheduling one for my 40th birthday. I was feeling better already.

Have you ever had times when you thought you were in control? Ha, I obviously tricked myself into thinking I was too, stressing over things I needed to let go and let God. We know God is sovereign. We know God is in control. Why do we put so much undue stress on ourselves sometimes? Is it just me who goes into worry mode and forgets the God I serve is bigger than any care I have? 1 Peter 5:7 reminds us to "Cast all your anxiety on him because he cares for you." "Who among you by worrying can add a single moment to your life?" Matthew 6:27 I've reminded myself of this one plenty of times in my life! Philippians 4:6 states "Don't be anxious about anything; rather, bring up all of your requests to God in your prayers and petitions, along with giving thanks." When you fully trust God, he knows your entire being - including everything you worry about and fear - and He's just waiting for you to ask Him to help you through it. How encouraging is Romans 16:20?! It triumphs "The God of peace will soon crush Satan under your feet." What worry or fear are you carrying around that you need to lay at the feet of the One who has already defeated fear?

DECEMBER 31

New Year's Eve came, and I was happy to spend it at home with just my boys although I keep planning next year's big events every time a holiday comes around. Next year, we'll go out and celebrate, painting the town red. Next year we'll host a giant party. Next year we'll do it up big. I'm looking forward to all those things while absolutely content with my current low-key celebrations this year. That night it laid down more ice and freezing rain. It was 2020's last revenge.

JANUARY 1

However, in the morning we woke up to the prettiest, most peaceful snowfall covering everything in sight. It felt like 2021 was telling us it was going to be ok. Overnight it took 2020's mess and turned it to beauty.

JANUARY 6

It was my 40th birthday and not only was I old, but I was bald and isolated too! This was not the bash I had pictured in my mind when I thought about celebrating my 40th. I wasn't sure if 40 would bother me, but I was happy to find out, it didn't! I woke up with ALL the joy that comes with every January 6. Chris ordered a yard sign declaring my elderly status to all the world. School wanted to have me on GMI live with them. It was awesome! My shirts came in and everyone was wearing them in a Punneo parade.

I also had my pre chemo appointment today because that's how 40-year old's celebrate, by going to the doctor. While I was waiting to go in, I was answering an email from a former student. She got in contact to wish me well and provide any help their family might be able to offer since they are no stranger to this disease. She's the sweetest. I had my appointment and glowed every time someone wished me happy birthday. As I was on my way out, I ran into the mom of the girl I was just emailing. What are the odds? I told her I was just in touch with her sweet girl. We talked a bit, shared our stories, and enjoyed each other's company. That's a big blessing to be able to converse with someone in a safe environment. That was God's way of giving me the equivalent of "coffee with a friend" on my birthday. I headed back home and decided to have my own version of a spa day complete with eye masks and a hot bath. While in my bath, I got my encouragement journal that Alexis compiled for me for Christmas. Because this thing was so big, I hadn't read through all of it yet. It was nice, as you contemplate your life for the first 40 years, to see that you have made a difference in people's lives so much so that they want to tell you, encourage you, and cheer you on for another 40. I read every last one and it was a fantastic way to spend a birthday. The shoot with Tenaciously Teal ended up not happening, but that was completely ok. I did, however, raise $500 for TT through a Facebook fundraiser. Wow! I had no idea that was going to happen when I first set it up. How amazing are my chemosabes?!? Alexis came over for dinner, Cheesecake Factory! Then, we watched the movie Soul together that just came out. I'm not sure if God is wanting me to rest assured I have made a difference with my life or prompt me to do something more and better, but He's given me a day to reflect on my life, what it means, and how to proceed moving forward. The day was a huge blessing full of joy.

I've learned the fruition of good reflection usually takes time. As I've gone back to re-read and relive these moments through the blessing of this book, I remember not understanding the path I was on or what purpose it had. I knew there was a plan, but it is only with the passing of time I can see it more clearly revealed. It took being steadfast in the hope of the Lord, open eyed to His will, and being obedient. Philippians 1:6 states "He who began a good work in you will carry it to completion until the day of Christ Jesus." God promised the Israelites a return from exile in Jeremiah 29:11 "For I know the plans I have for you, declares the Lord, plans to prosper you and not to harm you, plans to give you hope and a future." We can take encouragement from this as well when we feel like we are in times of exile during our journeys. Does the unknown bring anxiety? Rest assured there is something good coming. I never imagined this book was in my future at this time. God has a sense of humor for sure. If you were to dream your biggest dream for future plans in store for you, what would they be?

JANUARY 8

Chemo cycle 3 was today. I picked a chair by the window today and it was nice to have a view and sunshine. One of my options was my very first seat I had in chemo. Nope, no thank you. I had a new nurse and, of course, several attempts at an IV. Eventually a nurse, the hand IV master, got it in, but she kept asking why I didn't get a port. Because I don't want one, Karen! Do your job! Any who, we were able to get things going and I didn't have any back pains, but I did have a new, odd, marked reaction. Out of nowhere I felt a wave of intensity rising from my neck up. The best way I can describe it was like everything in my head suddenly became very thick, like everything expanded and got very dense by way of an extremely acute line rising. I told my FaceTime crew I was going to ring the bell and I did quickly. As my nurse started over she was asking what was wrong. I was trying to explain how my head was thick, but I couldn't finish before she figured it out. She burst out with, "Oh, you're flush!" Other nurses came over, did the vitals thing, stopped treatment, pushed other drugs, gave me oxygen, and waited it out with me, watching closely as I came out of whatever surprise that was.

I didn't like that one. I was used to back pains at this point. The feeling of your

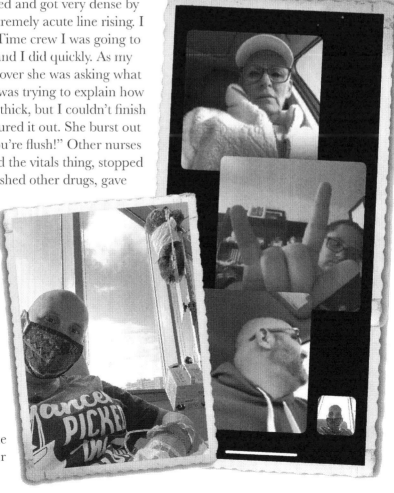

head changing forms is for the birds. We were able to get back to normal and start again without further incident, but I'd rather not do that again if I have the choice. Mom, Chris, and Luke were waiting for me as I left. Every chemo day they stay out in the parking garage close by for hours while I get treatment while FaceTiming so they can see what's going on as well. The side effects over the next week or so were basically mild. They included diarrhea, aches and pains, blood in my nose, loss of taste, a smorgasbord of saltines and Sprite for a few days, uneasiness of the stomach, and other things. I had my boys there every step of the way ready to help.

JANUARY 12

I went for my annual mammogram yesterday. They called today and said they saw something in my left breast and wanted to do more scans on the 19th to check it out further. I figured it was routine that this happens even in this case of it being nothing. At some point though, Chris and I had a talk, and he shared his concern about it being more serious, the cancer in general, and just his overall fear of losing me. He had every right to feel this way and confide in me about it, but something about that conversation got to me and made me worry a bit about this scare. I certainly didn't want to fight a 2-front battle with breast and ovarian cancer. The thought creeped into my head a bit. It never got to my heart. I trusted God every bit as much as I had before, but I felt a tiny bit of anxiousness waiting for new scans the next week. I didn't like it. I felt weaker than I should have KNOWING God had this whole thing in His hands.

JANUARY 15

Mom got me some fake magnetic lashes for Christmas, so I chose today to sport them. I Marco Polo'd Kort and Mom so they could see how fancy I was. They didn't go to waste either. I was able to don them out on the town at Walmart pickup. I knew the drop off guy as a friend's son. That poor kid had to look at me and not laugh while they flapped in the wind a bit. Also, another former student at the pharmacy drive thru was blessed by these bad boys waving in the wind. So, I have a lot to learn about the false eyelash world, but it was a good start. Lol.

JANUARY 19

New scans day for a more thorough mammogram. They squeezed extra hard to make sure they got a good picture of what they wanted. Luckily, I would get the results the same day so all I had to do was wait there for a bit. I had to go alone of course so I was waiting, maybe a little anxiously, and I get a text from Tori at church asking if there was anything she could pray for. I hadn't told anyone about this, so it was completely God's timing. Once again, the church was right there when I needed, even though they had no idea. (Just before Christmas, Clay and Jenny came by to deliver a beautiful pink poinsettia when Luke and I were rushing out to take Roger to the ER. It ended up being okay, but they were there ready to pray at just the right time then too). Between Clay checking in Halloween night when I was in the hospital parking lot at night with Chris in the ER, Clay and Jenny walking up to us as we're headed to the ER for Roger, and Tori checking in on me when I was waiting for these results, I'd say my God is present and working through my church. I'm thinking maybe they should quit checking in. Ha, maybe they are the common denominator!

I FaceTimed Mom and Kort for the results. The doctor didn't even come in. He just sent the nurse in to tell me all was well. It was just a scare, and I was all clear. Whew! All I have to do is fight ovarian cancer. All my focus can go into the current plan. I felt great after hearing that.

> "WHEN ANXIETY WAS GREAT WITHIN ME, YOUR CONSOLATION BROUGHT ME JOY." PSALM 94:19 "I SOUGHT THE LORD, AND HE ANSWERED ME; HE DELIVERED ME FROM ALL MY FEARS." PSALM 34:4 THESE ARE SUCH SIMPLE VERSES, BUT THEIR TRUTH PACKS IN SO MUCH HOPE. WHAT ARE YOUR GO TO VERSES FOR ENCOURAGEMENT? CREATE A COLLECTION OF VERSES YOU CAN SPEAK OVER YOUR LIFE, PRAY TO GOD, AND RECITE FOR COMFORT WHEN YOU NEED THEM. I ALSO MADE A PLAYLIST OF MY FAVORITE SONGS THAT ENCOURAGE ME AND SPEAK GOD'S TRUTH EVEN IF I'M ON THE GO.

JANUARY 22

I got a text from Amy saying this beautiful soul shaved her head for me. I don't even know her! I never had her in class. She's just an amazing human who shaved her head in support of me because that's the type of person she is. Can you even believe this? There are authentic people that love to do good and show good at every turn. Also, school was preparing for my next chemo day with shirts and support. IIS is the best!

JANUARY 26

The plan all along was to get scanned after my 3rd cycle of chemo to check on the progress or hopeful lack thereof of cancer in my torso. Since this cancer was so aggressive, we wanted to keep close tabs on any possible growth that could be happening and make sure the chemo was doing its job.

Today was the day I got to go and get another CT scan. This would make my 3rd CT of this journey, the first being the original that found the cancer on September 14, the second was after my first chemo in the ER on October 30, and this one - hopefully the least dramatic of all three! I would have to wait a couple of days to get the results, but I had zero worries. I'd also have to meet with one of Dr. Jackson's colleagues, because Dr. Jackson was on maternity leave for a while.

JANUARY 28

Chris was able to join me at this appointment because I was getting results. Woohoo for loopholes. Of course, we also FaceTimed Mom and Kort. We went in and talked with the new doctor who declared me still cancer free! There was no sign anywhere in my torso that the cancer had spread. Chemo was doing its job. We were working the plan and the plan was working. God has allowed healing and we were able to proceed with the plan at hand. Finish the last three rounds of chemo and check again with a CT. This relieved a lot of Chris's stress to know we were improving and moving in the exact direction we wanted. We see God's faithfulness and confirming that the peace and faith He placed in us from the beginning is never lost.

Because Dr. Jackson was on her maternity leave, we saw another doctor for this appointment. She was great, but she confirmed that God placed us in Dr. Jackson's care on purpose. The fill in doctor said she wouldn't have called for 3-month scans. She also eluded she was more laissez faire in her treatment style. We love Dr. Jackson and her treatment plan. Without these scans, Chris would've been stressed deluxe and inadvertently placed more stress on me. We had to wait on God's timing to get her, but she was worth it all. Another reminder God is in charge of every detail in this whole journey.

We got to spread the good news the rest of the day telling others of God's faithfulness. Woohoo!!

JANUARY 29

Round 4 of chemo. I was getting less excited about each chemo and this one I for sure wasn't looking forward to. For some reason I only got 3 hours of sleep last night, but still had a ton of energy and excitement when I got up and around. Maybe just knowing we get to keep our plan going and the end is in sight helped. I got to guest star on GMI this morning where they let me talk to the girl who shaved her head for me. What a girl of character and resolve!

Before chemo started we were able to bless Amy as she was waiting outside the Edmond OU for Todd to be scoped and evaluated. We stopped by and gave her Cheetos and Coke to get her through the lonely waiting. I think she appreciated it.

When Luke, Mom, and I got to the 3rd level in the parking garage, we decided to make a video to encourage random dancing. I figured I might need some cheering up during chemo today. Spoiler alert: no one sent any in, but I'll be on them next time. Lol!

I got in there and they had a hard time starting my IV again. They said Taxotere can be hard on veins. Mine are so small to begin with, it's getting more difficult as they go. This time the first nurse blew one up and missed another one. The second nurse, the hand master, the one who always tries to talk me into a port, looked, but when I showed her the scar she left on me from last time, she said she had another nurse that could do it with a shorter needle. Third nurse enters and gets it going. Whew!

This was the best chemo experience yet! We did stop due to some slight back pains. Really I just felt them starting but they never got to the point of pain. I caught Dee, my first nurse who epi penned me. She knew it was me and didn't take any chances, so she decided to stop it. We were able to continue, and I ended up getting some rest and had an overall great experience in treatment. What a blessing!

FEBRUARY 3

Ugh, this was the first day I really felt bad in an overall general yuck kind of way. I've dealt with acute issues, but today was a not get out of bed unless you're in the bath kind of low. It hit like a ton of bricks and I spent most of the day in bed. It did get better, but I'm tasting the impact of chemo - rather not tasting. Digestive grossness and major loss of taste came. I was super unhappy about all of it while trying to make the most of my saltine and Sprite smorgasbord. Also, my fingernails started hurting this time around some. This was the worst cycle for side effects yet. At least I'm on my 4th out of 6th round! Apollo came by to help make me feel better and it worked! He was my turning point and I think he needed me too.

FEBRUARY 17

Today I was supposed to go get my lab work and pre chemo appointment taken care of for cycle 5. Yesterday they called and said I would need to do my appointment with my nurse virtually due to TWO back-to-back "once in a decade" snowstorms. The temperatures here have been below zero for a week with wind chills down to -30. Snow totals are about 12 inches. Roads are bad and scary, and people have been in their houses dripping their faucets night and day. I think it's God's way of telling people to stay home and kick this COVID thing once and for all. Anyways, I checked to make sure the lab would still be open. Two different people said yes two different times. Today I had Bill drive me to OU to get my lab work done in his 4-wheel drive Jeep. They have never been unclear when they said, "No lab work, no chemo." We make the treacherous trek there and the building is completely closed up. We get word that I can get lab work done at the ER, so we head over there. They tell me they have to admit me as a patient, and I'll be charged the $1,000-$3,000 fee of an ER visit. My virtual call with my nurse is nonexistent although I'm waiting in the ER for almost an hour trying to get some kind of answer. Technology apparently also has been affected for some reason. Ugh, we finally made it home after this 4-hour scavenger hunt of trying to find someone to poke me with needles, but we got neither lab work or my appointment taken care of. A scheduler for the nurse called and rescheduled my appointment for a second time. She felt bad for not telling me they were closed when they found out at 7am the water wasn't working in the building, so she gave me her cell and told me to call before heading out to try for labs in the morning. Everywhere you look people's pipes are bursting due to this extended frigid weather we're just not used to and not built for.

FEBRUARY 18

I called her at 7:30 and Stephenson Cancer Center was still closed. Dang. Today is also the day I'm supposed to start my pre chemo Dexamethasone steroids. I wasn't sure if I should take it given the circumstances, but then it hit me what a huge lack of faith that was. I immediately swallowed those pills with a strong "In Jesus' mighty name!" even though on the surface, things were not looking good.

My virtual appointment was rescheduled again for 11:00. I'm at home this time and it worked well. The nurse said the plan was to come in in the morning and be ready for labs at 7:00. I'll continue to my chemo appointment after that. Whew, I'm still on track as long as Stephenson can open tomorrow. My prayer warriors came through again. Now we just need this building to be fixed and open today.

I also asked her about the end game. I had anticipated going back to school at the beginning of April, but needed to know what to expect as far as testing, appointments, and such. She asked if anyone had talked to me about maintenance treatment. I said no. She said a doctor would have to tell me about it, but it could be IV infusions every three weeks (sounds familiar), a daily pill, or multiple other options. I was ready to wrap this thing up and put a pretty bow on it after my next CT shows no more cancer. The last thing I thought about was more treatments, but God knew about this part too. I will trust in His plan.

FEBRUARY 19

For the first time in my life, I didn't sleep. At all, not even a wink. I just laid in bed thinking about all kinds of minor things wishing I was dreaming about them. But the good news was I got my outfit all planned out for chemo down to the shoes. I guess I worried about chemo not happening. Maybe I was worried about it happening. I don't know. I didn't feel worried. It wasn't in my head really, but I guess it affected my sleep. I'm not sure what else it could've been. Little did I know today would be a record setting kind of day. I ended up getting out of bed with Chris about 4. We watched the weather and road conditions for a bit. We'd be great there. It was finally going to reach 32 degrees after 2 weeks of brutally cold temps wreaking havoc on almost everything. I ate Raisin Bran as one last chance to pump up my Magnesium. I texted and called my nurse/scheduler friend again to see if Stephenson would be open. As we were leaving she called me back and said we were a go! Hallelujah! We got there with no issues in Bill's Jeep. Luke even went even though he told me it was too early for him yesterday. He likes to surprise me. I love that kid. I was second in line for labs about 10 till 7. I asked if they could just put the IV in so I could get stuck less, but, of course, that didn't fly. I finished and headed to chemo a few minutes early for my 7:30 appointment. It wasn't until after 9 that I was called back. I knew the labs would hold me up and they were very busy trying to make up missed days, so it was even longer. Eventually Dee picked me up. I was excited to get her again. The first thing she said as we were walking back was "I will never forget you or that day." Ha, the people that were there usually say that. She also always comments on the Cancer Buster gear Mom and I wore. We are impression makers if nothing else!

After pulling out all the tricks for my veins (the warm towels, lots of assessing, and finally deciding to go straight to the girl who got it last time with her special needles), we got it first time with only one stick! Another praise! Although Dee asked about me getting a port this time. Oh, the betrayal! However, she made up for it when she gave me a warm towel to put over my IV when I mentioned the premeds hurt going in sometimes. The warm towel opens them up.

Kort FaceTimed me to pray with me before chemo. I didn't FaceTime her before I went in because I knew she had the day off and I wanted to let her sleep in. That was kind of a blessing too because you can't be very discreet FaceTiming in there so a solid group of people got to hear one of Kort's amazing prayers!

She also got to watch the premeds go in over FaceTime and meet Dee too. Taxotere started about 11. Dee titrated it even more today making it take 3hours 45min now just for the Taxotere, but it worked! I had absolutely no side effects for the first time in the history of ever. In fact, even the premeds didn't hit as hard. I wasn't super thirsty, had no vision problems, the Benadryl didn't even hit that hard. It did tip the scales a bit though and I was able to get a light 45-minute nap in. Sleep felt good.

While I was there I thought I'd ask Dee about these possible IV treatments every 3 weeks and what I could expect if I needed those. She said they take just about 30 minutes to an hour to infuse. When I asked how long I'd have to take them, she obviously said everyone is different, but some take it indefinitely. When I asked about my veins and how hard that was on them she sadly said it was hard and gave me a look that I knew meant port. She also said it was probably the steroids that were keeping me from sleeping before chemo lately. Duh, of course! How else do I get little to no sleep and get up dancing??

By 4:00 I was out of there, just a short 9-hour day at Stephenson, but I was more than willing given I got out of bed with no idea if it was even going to happen at all. Praise God! Chemo cycle 5 out of 6 was in the books on schedule.

Think about all you have overcome so far in your journey. Have you thanked God for it? Take time to give the Lord from whom all good things come a little love. Make a list and thank Him for each one specifically. Even on your worst days you can go to this list and realize there was good, there is good, and there will be good to come. You know you didn't make it through all that alone. I know there have been moments when it was too much to handle. That is where God met you and took it from you. He never said you can do it all. He said when you can't handle it, lean on Him and He will comfort you and fight for you. Psalm 73:26 states "My flesh and my heart may fail, but God is the strength of my heart and portion forever."

FEBRUARY 25

This cycle has been overall very mild especially when compared to the last one. I've had some acid reflux when it comes to eating leafy greens. Apparently, chemo does not like them despite me needing the magnesium. I'm always trying to eat magnesium and potassium so my levels will be good enough for chemo, but those will have to wait for a week or so. I had some diarrhea towards the end, but everything was very mild. I anticipated each round getting worse as the effects culminated, but this was a very pleasant surprise.

I've always thought I checked the box next to the bougie cancer experience. Every aspect could have been so much worse and has been for so many others. I look at Todd and his journey unfolding and know I have it easy. I am incredibly blessed, and I am thankful for it. One such blessing I've allowed myself to enjoy is an in-home massage after every chemo cycle. I have it timed so that it's at the peak of aches and pains, about a week after chemo. I feel like it not only feels amazing in the midst of aches and pains, but it also loosens that chemo in my body and is another way to work it out of my system, releasing those toxins. My masseuse is super clean which I love! She's the only outsider I let into my bubble. She wipes down everything before, including her phone, she wears a mask at all times, her sheets smell so clean, she wipes down everything after, and she works in a clinic, so she knows medical grade cleanliness and protocol. It is a perk and part of the bougie cancer package. This picture depicts the Tibetan monk I found in the mirror before this cycle's massage. LOL! Also included in the bougie cancer package was a house cleaner. Mine was supposed to come again right when I got COVID and be a regular every month, but I decided to not have someone come in and touch every living surface in the house so that only lasted once. Otherwise, she would be here. That was something I'd always wanted.

The fact that I could spend this time at home, not working, but keeping my job is monumental to my stress-free recovery. The fact that chemo has been manageable is a blessing I didn't expect. You hear some of the worst stories and I anticipated death warmed over most days. I think that's why I'm always impressed with how "mild" my side effects are. Perspective is everything and being warned with the worst can be a silver lining. There are so many details I can think of that have made this journey a true blessing in so many respects.

MARCH 2

Today was a beautiful day outside. I've been eyeing my couch to 10K program but have been scared to even think about it given my long stretch of inactivity. I know I'm far behind where I normally am and that's usually behind too! I decided to go out and give it a try. It starts easy enough and I needed it to. I was just hoping my body could make it. I still have one chemo treatment left so I won't be able to start without taking breaks from the program, but I know I'm close and starting it now can only help.

I tell you what, I wanted to jump for joy when I started running. I wanted to scream "I'm running!" to people outside. It was only a minute at a time, but it absolutely wore me out. My legs were jello while simultaneously heavy as tree trunks, but I did it! This was a tiny physical feat, but a huge mental one in which I realize I need to start training, but it's going to be a long hard road ahead. I Facebooked it afterwards and my chemosabes were amazing. I hate to say it, but I wanted their celebrations. I wanted to rejoice with someone. As always, they came through and were super encouraging.

Also -TMI alert- as I showered I realized I had lost all hair. Eventually everything fell out. I felt like a 6-year-old girl. The other day I wondered why my arms were so soft. I realized I had no arm hair anymore. All that's left are some thin eyebrows and eyelashes. The hair on my head is patchy, but I still shave it every few days. It's the only hair still growing. I wondered in the beginning if I shaved

> Rachel Dawn Punneo
> 19h
>
> Well, I did it! I poured my extra 13 pounds of hysterectomy sabotaged, 40 year old, cancer fighting, chemoed body in my old running attire for the first time in many months. With a letting out of the ol sports bra and tie around my shorts, I set out around the neighborhood. But I did it. I finished the first run of couch to 10K. It was so hard. My legs were like jello. But I did it. Pray that this is the first of many to come, Chemosabes! Side perk: I didn't have to take my wet nasty hair out of a tie afterward! Winning!
> Can I just give a shout out to my amazing husband right now too?!? He tells me I'm beautiful though scarred. He tells me I'm beautiful while giant and pregnant. He tells me I'm beautiful when I was hot! He's told me I'm beautiful at each and every phase of my journey because, well, he's been around for all those phases. I hope every girl is as lucky as I am to feel so beautiful in their husband's eyes no matter the time in life.

I WAS NOT LYING WHEN I SAID POURED IN. MY CUP RUNNETH OVER IN MANY FORMS!

my head for nothing, but it's clear it would've just come out slowly and in spots. Had I tried to keep it, I would've looked really sick. Since I shaved it, I've really liked it though. Chris liked it, my chemosabes were so complimentary, and you feel proud of your journey, full of strength, moxie, and grit. Growing it out may be a different story, but while I'm bald, I'm finding the perks!

MARCH 4

I cried. All. Day. Long. I didn't even know a person could cry all day. I woke up and weighed myself. I gained TWO pounds in one day. That's 15 pounds gained since the beginning of this whole process.
That's the biggest I've been in my life with the exception of one of my pregnancies - not even both. I don't know that I'll ever be able to lose this weight over 40. I cleaned out the shelter and cried the whole time. Teardrops were all over the bottom. I went on a walk to the lake and sat there for a while watching the waves crash at my feet. I cried the whole time. I took Luke to Walmart. I cried the whole time in the parking lot. I cried while doing dishes. I cried talking to the Mathis Brothers lady about our mattress. I cried in the shower. I cried all day. So much for "I'm not much of a crier." I don't know where that came from. I've never done that before in my whole life.

I gave myself today. I don't know that I really had a choice otherwise, but I know I've only had a couple days so far I needed to take to be sad and they were both for COVID. Today was a day I needed to be sad for these circumstances. I needed to cry. Chris came home and held me and made me feel better.

It amazed me at how positive I'd been so far with all this to come crashing down in a blubbering mess all of a sudden. Where did this come from? Even while crying I didn't know why I was crying. It was like the worst period cry ever and when someone asks why you're sobbing, you snivel, "I don't knoooow!" and cry some more about that.

Who knew cancer would make you gain weight? That blindsided me. I even thought at the beginning of this that would be one of the few perks to this...I'd lose weight. False. Between extreme inactivity (rest before surgery so I didn't tweak Helga, rest after surgery, rest with chemo, being isolated in the bedroom with COVID, crazy winter weather), insta-menopause with the hysterectomy, steroids, crazy out of whack hormones, and turning 40, this was a perfect storm of weight gain.

MARCH 5

Chris hid my scale from me.

MARCH 11

I rescheduled my pre chemo appointment so I could talk with a doctor about this whole maintenance treatment business. It was throwing a wrench into my plans for going back to school and wrapping this up in a nice neat little bow. I was scheduled to see the fill in doctor again.

Because all research done and studies shown were for stage 2 and above, no information was available for how maintenance treatment would affect me at a 1B. The general consensus was that it'd do more harm than good and none of the doctors she passed it by wanted to take that risk especially since I didn't have the gene for it. Although my official chances are 20% of a future recurrence, she also said she didn't expect to see me back ever again. What fantastic news!! I'd be done with this after one last chemo tomorrow!

I asked about the COVID vaccine again since I was free to return to school. Again, they said they recommended it. I checked the ingredients versus Taxol, and she said nothing was related. I would get it there at OU and they would watch me for 30 minutes afterwards. This part still makes me a little nervous. I just don't want to put any new things in my body, but it does give us some freedom that we haven't had in a very long time.

I asked about my crying bout and where that came from. She said it was probably from hormones. Sometimes it takes a while for those symptoms to manifest. Also, my numbing nose and legs are fine while running as long as it goes away. I definitely asked about drinking too. Not that I'm a big drinker, but it's been a long time since October, and I drink delicious drinks so I'm looking forward to getting something tasty to celebrate! Mom and I already have plans for bushwhackers very soon.

Overall, I left the appointment ecstatic. No more treatment, no port, and I can go back to school when I want. God is so good. I have no idea why He graced me with such a charmed cancer experience, but I'm coming out on the other side not much worse for wear. Thank you, Lord!

I talked with Amy about returning to school later that night. While I was initially thinking April 2 or so, I knew I had appointments up to April 14th now so I should wait to come back until then, so I wasn't taking time off right away. She suggested waiting until May 1 to give me time to recover and build up stamina. I love that she looks after me.

MARCH 12

As I was heading out for my last chemo treatment and the garage door opened, I noticed some legs in the yard. As I was wondering who was in my yard, I realized there was a whole slew of people out there ringing bells and cheering for me. What a surprise! Some of the staff came by to send me off with the best support. Mind you this was their first day of Spring Break and they had conferences late last night. My school is the best!

Today was a spectacular day all around. Danielle, my long-term sub, even made me a video from my class wishing me good luck. Kortney came down to celebrate the momentous occasion too. We met her at OU, and I got to hold her hand while she prayed one of those amazing prayers. It just wouldn't have been the same without her there.

At chemo, my IV was in with the first shot and it was in my left arm, so it was comfortable and not in the way at all. I got a congratulatory cupcake from a volunteer since it was my last treatment. I don't think Dee was really my official nurse today, but she made sure to come over, talk to me, and take care of me like she was my own. I gave her more brain books for her mom and she asked how I knew the Graces since we've been connecting through Facebook. I had no reactions!

A sweet funny 96-year-old patient was my neighbor again. She is the best. I hope I can be a beam of light like her at that age. I asked what her best advice was, and she said, "to be a lady."

At one point she looked up at Flash hanging off my IV pole, looked a little confused and screamed (because that's how she always talked), "Is that someone's wig? Did someone leave their hair up there?" I had to explain that it was Flash. He has certainly made his presence known there. A nurse came by and said she was going to miss seeing him hanging around after I was gone. The people at OU are great.

As you can see, after chemo was over I met up with my entourage on the lower level of Stephenson to find that elusive bell, the bell that declares you are done with treatment, a definite rite of passage for all fighters if you get the opportunity to ring it. Luckily, the security guard let them all in. I think he thought they all had to go to the bathroom again. Either way they rushed through and made it to the bell with me! I didn't know that anyone would make it down with me so I planned to Facebook Live it so others could join in with me to close this journey out together. I had to do something to make it a little less anti-climactic. Luckily, Luke was there to video. There were people clear down the hall cheering and screaming for me too as I rang it. You'll never hear me doubt there's good in people, even perfect strangers.

Kort also had some ideas. She had me pack my robe and gloves so I could come out to a Carrie Underwood song in fighter's fashion. It worked out though that she could video me punching out the bell and video me all the way down the hall since she got in. We did it once and it didn't record. Lol, the lady behind the desk laughed at us. We shot it a second time and we got it. I should've planned it out more and had better moves, learned the words, and had my hood up in the beginning, but it was a lot of spontaneous fun and I'm so glad Kort was there to make it happen. Everyone should have a walkout moment after their last chemo.

Mom drove me home and I relaxed most of the night with the boys. Looking over Facebook was such a delight. Everybody was sharing the good news! It felt like a good way to close out our journey together.

MARCH 13

In the coming days, I was much more tired starting earlier and lasting longer. My nose wasn't nearly as bloody inside as it usually is with each cycle. As the end came my diarrhea got bad. Butt cream was bought. That is all I will divulge on that. My fingernails took a toll with them being very brittle, tender, and feeling as though they're detaching. My red cheeks lasted much longer than I thought as well. I was down to the last time I'd be sending Mom and Kort pictures of my tongue, lol. However white it became each round was a sign of how gross I usually felt and how much my taste had gone. My BioTene could be packed up soon too.

MARCH 22

I feel like today is a turning point. I'm rounding the corner on side effects and coming out the other side for the last time. It feels like a new beginning.

Luke went to school for the first time in months today. It makes me a little sad, but he's only been to the high school a month or so since starting in August, so I guess it's time. He says he remembers where his classes are.

I talked with Amy today about coming back. It looks like we compromised on April 26. This will be after testing so the kids don't have to transition with me while worrying about their first ever B.U.T. That's what I call the state test required at the end of the year, the Big Ugly Test. They can take it with Danielle who they're comfortable with. I will be their monitor though! I'll start to creep in their lives little by little. Amy was protective about me being able to recover and be ready for this which is just one reason why I love her, but I feel good about a return date on the 26th.

Chris and I were talking today about making sure Luke knew he was released from protecting me and could be free to live his life again and get back out there. We want to make sure he knows that and that I should probably start taking steps to show him that I'm better too. I realized returning to school this year is a definite part of my recovery more so than I could previously identify. I think if I didn't return this year, this whole COVID, cancer, chemo experience would just elongate into summer making it one big break eventually slamming hard into next August. If I go back this year, it provides some closure to the experience and summer can be well earned and feel like a summer break, not an extension of the whole process I've gone through. And it symbolizes to Luke that his mom is back and normal and it's ok to be a kid again. I see light at the end of the tunnel.

Also, today I got a Tropical Smoothie and it tasted delicious! I mean delicious! I knew my taste was completely back and realized I had probably lost my taste for the last time! Hallelujah! That brings such a smile to my soul.

> New beginnings are filled with such hope and joy. Isaiah 43:18-19 states "Forget the former things; do not dwell on the past. See, I am doing a new thing! Now it springs up; do you not perceive it? I am making a way in the wilderness and streams in the wasteland." You see God is the creator of new beginnings. He literally created everything in the first beginning, and he has the power and love to grant us do overs daily because, let's face it, we need them. In Lamentations 3:22-23 we find these incredible words: "Because of the Lord's great love we are not consumed, for his compassions never fail. They are new every morning; great is your faithfulness." The God of this universe is so faithful and loving to care about us trying to get it right. How blessed are we to serve a God that allows us mulligans every single day and give us the hope that comes with it? A big new beginning is right around the corner for you too. What are you going to do with it? Does knowing God's great faithfulness drive that hope within you even more?

MARCH 23

    I went to my PCP and started on my plans with her to get better. I asked about hair regrowth and getting my gut in shape. Through all this, I realized life is too short to feel bad. She referred me to a gastroenterologist and suggested I start on Rogaine for men to get my hair back on track. I talked to her about getting the vaccine as well. She suggested it. I'm not sure why, but as I was talking to her about it, I started to get emotional. She asked if I was depressed, lol. I told her I really was great through this whole ordeal, but I was worried about any possible reactions. She gave me a Valium for the morning I was going to get vaccinated just to help.

MARCH 25

    Although I was nervous, I went to get my COVID shot at CVS. The doctor's office called a few days ago and said I wouldn't get my shot at OU, that it would be at a different location through IMMY, so I found a location through CVS closest to the ER I like that had a nurse and EpiPen at the ready. I showed up, waited in line, and asked to see the nurse. There wasn't one there despite what they told us. I backed out. I did not feel comfortable getting one without some type of medical support. The rest of the day was supposed to be filled with day drinking with Mom as a celebration of me surviving the shot and finishing chemo. Instead a couple of family members talked to me about possibly not getting the shot. I'm not going to lie. It rattled me and I didn't go to my newly rescheduled shot on Monday either.

MARCH 30

    I found out a friend from school went into anaphylactic shock at her second COVID shot and had to be rushed to the hospital. It was a very scary moment for her that I know all too well. I talked with her some and decided to dig deeper into the ingredients of both the vaccine and Taxol. What I found was shocking. Dr. Jackson always said I was allergic to the solvent in the Taxol. I investigated the solvent closer and found that the major component in the solvent is the same PEG that the CDC warns against taking the vaccine if you're allergic to. In fact, that's about the only reason they warn you against taking the vaccine. I didn't know about this when I initially read about it because it went by a different name. If I had gone through with the vaccine I really feel like I would've been on the CVS floor in no time.

Had I not had cancer and treated it with Taxol initially, I never would've known about this allergy. As it was, I was able to be treated in the Stephenson Center with dozens of nurses there within seconds, an IV already in and meds pushed immediately, paramedics there in no time, and all the help a person could need, and it was still touch and go for a while.

If I never would've gone through that -in the safest possible manner- I never would've known I had this allergy. If I never had cancer, I probably would've got my shot in some Walmart and been on the floor with no idea why and help not close enough.

I am so thankful for my cancer and experience. It very well could've saved my life. It gave me a breather year from teaching, possibly an unrealized much needed break to let me revive and rejuvenate after going so hard for so long. This year could've been the breaking point with all that changed.

THE PHRASE GOD WORKS IN MYSTERIOUS WAYS IS NOT NEW TO YOU I'M SURE. MAYBE I'M JUST MAKING UP THESE ALTERNATE REALITIES, BUT I REALLY DO FEEL LIKE CANCER SAVED ME IN MANY WAYS ON MANY LEVELS I NEVER COULD'VE ORCHESTRATED MYSELF. IN ROMANS 11:33-36, WE GET THIS INSIGHT. "OH, THE DEPTH OF THE RICHES OF THE WISDOM AND KNOWLEDGE OF GOD! HOW UNSEARCHABLE HIS JUDGEMENTS AND HIS PATHS BEYOND TRACING OUT! WHO HAS KNOWN THE MIND OF THE LORD? OR WHO HAS BEEN HIS COUNSELOR? WHO HAS EVER GIVEN TO GOD, THAT GOD SHOULD REPAY THEM? FOR FROM HIM AND THROUGH HIM AND FOR HIM ARE ALL THINGS. TO HIM BE THE GLORY FOREVER! AMEN." I THINK OF JOSEPH AND HOW LONG HE LIVED IN THE MYSTERY OF WHY HIS BROTHERS SOLD HIM. THAT COULDN'T HAVE MADE ANY SENSE TO HIM. LIFE MAY NOT MAKE SENSE NOW TO YOU EITHER. MAYBE IT WON'T UNTIL WE STAND BEFORE OUR CREATOR DIRECTLY, BUT KNOW WHATEVER HAPPENS, GOD'S GOT YOU. WHAT IS IT THAT MAKES THE LEAST SENSE TO YOU THROUGHOUT THIS JOURNEY? FOR FUN, WHAT'S THE WILDEST EXPLANATION YOU CAN COME UP WITH TO MAKE IT WORK OUT FOR YOUR GOOD?

MARCH 31

My 127 sick days were going to be depleted on April 20. With coming up a little short and knowing I had multiple appointments ahead of me still, I asked for days to be donated. Chris had me ask for the max of 100 although that felt very greedy. I followed his advice for 3 reasons: I learned you can never predict what the future holds, you can't request any more donated days for 2 years, and it would be more feasible to decline or give back days than to get more. Also, I could always pay it forward if I was stuck with them. An email was sent out and days could be donated through April 6. Today I learned the max amount of days were donated. One friend texted me and said they would only let her donate a third of what she wanted to. Another said her school was all trying to give me days, but it filled up so fast. Can you believe that? This whole time I've said I was enjoying my year of early retirement since I had to use all my days I was so careful to acquire. Now, I've recovered the majority of them. When I knew I could request days, I was just thinking I would get by this year and hopefully have enough to cover appointments in the future. Now, I am blessed with being able to breathe on that front. I didn't take as hard of a hit as I thought because of the generous people of YPS. I wish I could see who donated and thank them personally. Wow, another major blessing to add to the list.

APRIL 2

I started to get out a bit and we went to Uncle Mike's birthday party. I stayed outside 97% of the time. I only went in for a few pictures, one of which was this doppelganger pic. It was a nice way to ease back into the world.

APRIL 4

Easter came and I am reminded again about Jesus's love for me and how He wants the very best for my life in Him. He has never steered me wrong yet. He has been faithful. I've trusted in Him this whole process and I've never been let down by it. He has given me peace and strength to endure it all. I thank God for my healing and give Him all the glory.

We were able to celebrate Resurrection Day with dying eggs, resurrection rolls, egg hiding, and an Easter dinner at Mom's. We played Putterball and I had my first drink since October. Mom made bushwhackers and it was delicious.

APRIL 8

It was B.U.T. day at school and I got to monitor for all of pod D. Because this year was different, one person could monitor multiple classes. I brought Starbucks to the office staff and pod D as a thank you. As I walked into the vestibule with 11 drinks I got a little teary eyed. It was the first time I've been there since September 11. I had no idea when I walked out that day I wouldn't be back there until now. It was a little emotional being back in my second home and seeing so many genuinely happy faces. When I got in, Star came right up to me and declared "I need a hug!" I was honored. Star does not give hugs. In fact, that's my go to threat with her if I need something. "Don't make me give you a hug!" Lol. It was the best greeting ever and my day was already made!

I got to be on GMI in person and it was fantastic and fun. I delivered Starbucks and smiled at every new person I saw. I went into pod D and each class clapped for me and cheered as I went in. My heart was beating

so fast, and I got hot from excitement. Well, that and hot flashes. I told everyone I was the most excited test monitor they've ever had. It was so good for my soul. I tried not to hug too many people, not as many as I wanted to, but the ones I did hug were amazing. As one of my first times out in the real world, I didn't want to be too overwhelmed with full body touching hundreds of people. I didn't hug kids, but some staff came with arms open wide and I didn't want to miss out on their love. I think it was needed both ways. My feet hurt by the end of the day. I haven't been on them that long since last March! It was a happy hurt though. I went home with my heart full.

APRIL 12

Dinner was a non-existent thing tonight, so we ended up going out to eat. For the first time since October, I went to a restaurant. Granted, it was a patio (baby steps), but it felt great to get out a bit. We went to Fuzzy's to enjoy fresh nachos and I ended up getting a margarita to celebrate because I could.

My sweet former fourth grader, Snow, asked me a couple days ago if she could post an Instagram story on the district's page about me ringing the bell. I gave her a quote she asked for and it posted tonight. I shared it on FB from the district's page and boy did things start to take off! By the end of the night KOCO picked it up and put it on their online news.

APRIL 13

I woke up to several people telling me they saw me on the morning news not only on news 5, but also on news 9's broadcast. What?! More people had said they heard about me on Jake FM and the Twister. Lacie Lowry also posted me on her fb page. How crazy was this? As I checked my email, our district PR person told me People wanted videos of the bell ringing because they wanted to put me on their TV show. In less than 24 hours my bell ringing story had spread from now to People magazine! By the end of the night, I was reading about my story on People.com. The TV segment was going to air tomorrow night.

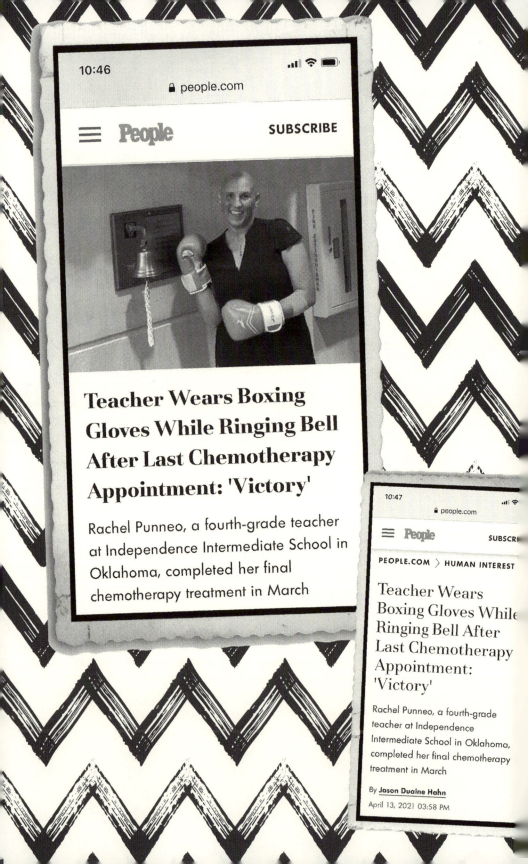

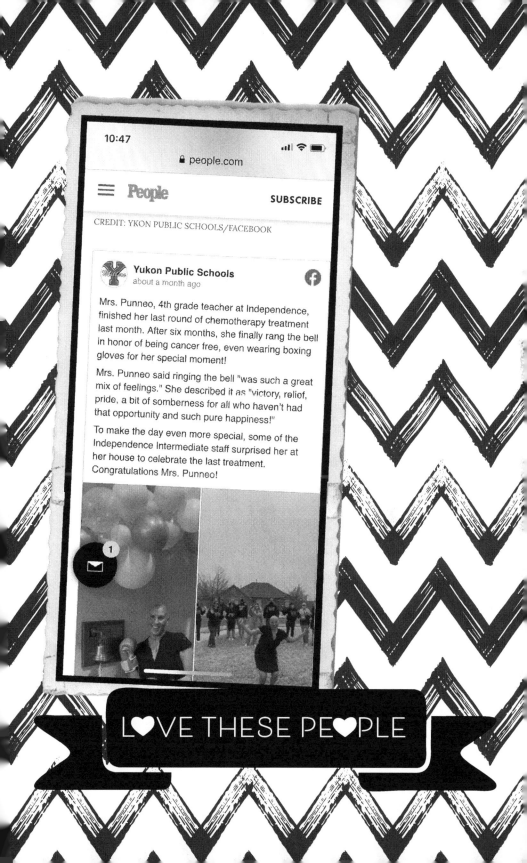

An elementary teacher from Oklahoma recently sported a pair of boxing gloves to her last round of chemotherapy, calling the experience a "great mix of feelings."

Rachel Punneo wore light blue boxing gloves as she celebrated ringing the bell at her last treatment of chemotherapy in March, Yukon Public Schools shared in a Facebook post. The fourth-grade teacher at Independence Intermediate School in Oklahoma also marked six months free of ovarian cancer.

"Mrs. Punneo, 4th grade teacher at Independence, finished her last round of chemotherapy treatment last month," Yukon Public Schools wrote on social media.

"After six months, she finally rang the bell in honor of being cancer-free, even wearing boxing gloves for her special moment," they added.

In the post, the district said Punneo called the moment "a great mix of feelings."

"She described it as 'victory, relief, pride, a bit of somberness for all who haven't had that opportunity and such pure happiness!'" the district wrote.

Celebrating the milestone, a few members of the school even made an appearance outside Punneo's home.

"To make the day even more special, some of the Independence Intermediate staff surprised her at her house to celebrate the last treatment," the district's social media post reads. "Congratulations Mrs. Punneo!"

On her Facebook page, Punneo thanked everyone who came out to celebrate with her.

"Today is a good day to have a good day. Leaving for chemo today I had the best cowbell ringers to teach me how to properly ring a bell," she wrote. "This is coming from the best teachers the world has to offer! What a fantastic surprise of support!"

"I'm telling ya, I love these guys!! The day only filled with more treasures," Punneo added. "Look through to see some of the good in this world!"

Punneo said even though she will have "many appointments to come," she can now look forward to life without treatment.

"This present that is cancer is about to get wrapped up in petty paper, a cute bow, and be punted to the curb with much enthusiasm!" she wrote in a previous social media post. "I will be done."

APRIL 14

I had to go get bloodwork and go to see Dr. Jackson for my final(ish) appointment. I was really excited to see her. It was supposed to be her first day back, but she wasn't there. I was bummed, but I spoke with the nurse instead. She said my scans were clear! It was a non-issue in my book. I knew that already, but Praise God for it! She did say though that I had a sac of fluid about 6cm by 6cm that is by my bladder. It was from surgery, and they knew about it and have been watching it shrink little by little. I didn't know that, but for now that's what I'm blaming these extra 15 pounds on. ;) She said it would slowly take care of itself, so it was nothing to worry about. The name Sacajawea seemed fitting for her since she was on my bladder. She also said I could start growing my hair out anytime. So long, beautiful bald head! Hello, awkward growing out stages!

I also wanted to confirm exactly what I was allergic to. Was it specifically the PEGs or just Taxol altogether? The nurse called in the pharmacist who was smart and approachable. We talked and I shared my findings with her. She said I was probably fine. She was 99% sure I'd be fine getting the vaccine, but she'd do some research and get back with me.

At the same time, I was in my appointment, Todd was a couple floors down ringing the bell celebrating being done with his 65 rounds of hard-core radiation.

Hallelujah! I wanted to make it down and cheer for him, but I was stuck in the office. Too bad. As Amy said, "so close, but so many doors in between."

That night my episode on People TV aired. It came right after a Fast and the Furious story with Vin Diesel and John Cena. How crazy is this? My name was even in the credits. I'm not sure why, but that was very exciting too!

APRIL 15

Amy called this morning and let me know we were official for starting back on the 26th. Danielle and I would co teach for the first week so if I needed to take the afternoon off or take some breaks she would be there to help. Since Danielle was hired as an intern the rest of the year she would be around to fill in for anyone at Independence or Lakeview, but I always had priority so if I woke up and felt like I couldn't handle it, Danielle came to me first no matter where she may have been scheduled. I can't tell you how much I love Amy and how she's had my back every step of the way despite her own journey she's trudging through.

The pharmacist called and said she had mixed feelings about me getting the vaccine after really diving into my case and doing deep research. She went back and looked at my unique batch of Taxol I used that day, the solvent used, got the identification numbers for those, checked specifically for the type of particular PEGs within that batch, and concluded the vaccine wasn't for me. She said I could be just fine taking it, but she wasn't a risk taker and for my safety she couldn't recommend it though she has for most other people. I felt so much better after that. I told her I felt so many people have just given me the generic "Get the vaccine" spiel without really considering my situation. I was so glad she was there to give me an honest and intelligent opinion. Looks like I'll be continuing to wear masks, distance, and wash my hands with fervor for a long time still. I'm ok with that.

An hour or so later I checked my FB and some new person I didn't know said she PM'd me. I've had so many friend requests since this whole journey began and especially in the past couple days since this story got traction. In fact, one of my 3rd graders found me. I didn't get to see her for her graduation last year because of COVID. She told me she's going to school to be a pediatrician. I love that so many have reached out and this has served as a tool to reconnect with so many.

With that, many strangers have got in touch too. I've been a little leerier of contacting them. I checked my message though and I was completely shocked. It was Brenna from the ELLEN show! My mouth dropped. TMI - I was sitting in the bathroom and looked down at my Ellen undies I was sporting at the time and laughed once I was able to move again.

What is happening in this insane world of mine? After I showed Luke and FaceTimed Tawnie I quickly responded to her through email. We were going to zoom tomorrow for a "preliminary chat". Mind blown.

APRIL 16

We zoomed for over 40 minutes! It was nice to be asked about everything and info not just passed along. Brenna was super peppy and sweet just like you would expect someone on Ellen's staff to be. She said I was "a ray of sunshine." (Sometimes I still have to remind Chris loudly "I am a ray of sunshine!") If it never goes any further than this, I would be completely okay with it. To talk with Ellen's people for that long is a wild turn of events I never expected, and I'm excited I can count all this as part of my adventure.

Also, the pharmacist called back and said she did more research because I was on her mind. She said the Johnson and Johnson vaccine also wouldn't be recommended when it came back. Again, she said it could be fine, but she just wasn't super confident it wouldn't cause a reaction too.

APRIL 20

Today was the Math B.U.T. and I was able to monitor again. I came bearing Starbucks for my Care Team Committee and Math PLC this time. I was also able to talk to Danielle for a bit. She made me a whole binder full of information, a writeup on every student in my class, a welcome back letter, behavior trackers, and lesson plans for the rest of the year. I was so impressed by how much she cared and how much work she put in it to make sure I didn't have to worry about coming back.

APRIL 22

After sending in pics and videos, emailing back and forth, answering the most twilight zone questions (Do you have any financial hardships? Has anyone like The Today Show, Kelly Clarkson, or GMA contacted you for an interview? Since you're an Oklahoma gal, do you love Garth Brooks or Chris Stapleton?), and being asked if I was available today, Brenna emailed me and said they had their season pretty well booked, but would let me know if anything changed. Wow. Just wow.

It's hard to believe I even had a chance of being featured on the Ellen Show. While I would've loved to tell of God's goodness on a national platform like that, I'll just keep telling whoever will listen around here. The collateral beauty of this journey is beyond anything I could ever imagine! God is good all the time and all the time God is good!

APRIL 26

It's D-Day! My return to school finally came. Today was a bit of a rough day. The kids were nonstop talking and out of their formerly trained ways. I had a "come to Jesus" talk with my homeroom at the end of the day. I also changed up a few things before the next day to help with classroom management. Tuesday and the rest of the week saw improvements though they still aren't where I'd like them to be. My feet and legs were killing me to the point it hurt to walk at all at night. At the end of the week, I really went through and purged and cleaned. It felt so much better in there and I was super excited to refresh the room a bit and start by myself next week.

MAY 8

The past week of school certainly had its ups and downs. The positives were Teacher Appreciation week with dress up days, food trucks, and presents! I received one of my very favorite kid pictures of me ever and I also scheduled a lunch date with the amazing girl who shaved her head for ME! I got Cane's and we talked. She is so well spoken and has such a calming aura about her. I really loved my time with her. She told me she just really wanted to do something special for me. She truly is a special human.

The negatives were just as impactful. The mask mandate was lifted due to crazy parents protesting at the board meeting. Our superintendent even mentioned my situation at the meeting to which one person screamed, "She can stay home!" The meltdowns from the 4th grade humans were just as bad. One student screams and curses like an angry sailor. A couple are experts at throwing huge kindergarten tantrums. It's unlike anything I've dealt with before. Whew! I'm halfway there with 9 days down and 9 to go. I firmly believe I'll earn my summer break.

Jenny, our pastor's wife, asked me a couple weeks ago if I'd be willing to be the speaker at the church's Tea Party. I said yes and today was the day. I don't know that I hit it out of the park, but I did get to speak of God's goodness and how it was present in every minute detail of this journey. I was only supposed to speak for 10 minutes, and I went 20! ...and that was limited to the highlights. God is too good to be contained to just 10 minutes! ;)

Several people came to me afterward and said I was inspiring, or I did great, but they are very nice people. I think I did decently. Maybe I'll get another shot to spread the word. Maybe my whole life. I have it now to do with what I want. Here's hoping I can keep shining that light and pointing people in His direction with this story.

I tell you these things so that you may have peace. You will have troubles in this world, but take heart. I have overcome the world.

John 16:33

Dear Heavenly Father,

My father who is so good to me, thank you for this journey you allowed. Thank you for opening my eyes to the collateral beauty all around. Thank you for surrounding me with loved ones, enveloping me in your peace that passes understanding, and giving me joy even in the hard times. Thank you for letting me see glimpses of the whys along the journey. Thank you for taking care of even the minute details like t-shirts! I praise you for keeping me healthy and alive through even the scariest moments. You've shown me I'm worth living, I have more to do in this world, and you have me no matter the circumstances. Thank you for your protection from the top of my bald head to the bottom of my soles.

I am so grateful for the people you put in my path to encourage me through it all. My boys who took care of me day and night. Alexis, Mom, and Kortney who were always there at the drop of a hat if I needed anything. Amy, Tamara, and all of IKS who cheered me on and never forgot me. My whole village has been the best part of all of this, and you orchestrated each meet and each crossing of our paths. I praise you for the doctors, nurses, and medicine you provided.

Thank you for allowing this journey and allowing me to grow from it. Please help me to learn from it what you need me to learn. I don't want to waste this opportunity you gave me. Open my eyes to your future for me. Stir in my soul your plans and guide my feet.

You deserve all the glory for being in the fire with me, never leaving my side. I praise you for bringing me out of it, not even smelling of smoke! I love you, Lord, and I give you all the glory. Thank you for allowing me to be a vessel for you and shine your light in this way.

Amen

Epilogue:

And that's where my journal ended. Whew! Isn't it wild to read some of those things knowing that God provided in those situations and in big ways. When you look at the details of your journey, do you see God's fingerprints woven throughout? Since May God has blessed me with more adventures on this cancer journey. I have walked in a runway show at Tenaciously Teal's fundraiser event. Tenaciously Teal is an organization I'm proud to be a part of. They help cancer fighters with many services and uplift each one giving hope for another day. Check them out at TTeal.org. Through a crazy turn of events I have published the book in your hands. That was never on my radar. Cancer has added both runway model and published author to my resume. What a ride!

I would be remiss if I didn't try to share with you the source of hope and peace I was blessed with on my journey. If you haven't accepted Christ as your Savior, I want you to know He loves you so much. This life is hard, too hard to do by yourself. God gives his grace freely and shows mercy beyond what we deserve. You may have memorized John 3:16 which states "For God so loved the world that He gave his one and only son so whosoever believes in him shall not perish, but have everlasting life." Doesn't that sound nice? Pray a prayer inviting God to come into your life. Ask him to forgive your sins. You can repeat this prayer if you don't know what to say.

Dear Father,

Thank you for loving me so much that you gave your son because you couldn't stand the thought of eternity without me. I know I don't want to spend eternity without you. I know I have sinned. I'm sorry for that. Please forgive me. Send your gift of the Holy Spirit to help me and guide me. I love you and I thank you for saving me from myself and my earthly ways. Amen.

Thank you, chemosabe, for joining me on this journey.

Made in the USA
Coppell, TX
25 April 2022

77030760R00067